blue Monday

Absolute Beginners

CHAILÍN RUA
CHYNNA-2001

Chynna Clugston Flores
Writer & Illustrator

Jordie Bellaire
Colorist

Sean Konot
Letterer

Drew Gill
Book Design

Jamie S. Rich
First Edition Editor

Ian Shaughnessy
Remastered Edition Editor

BLUE MONDAY created by
Chynna Clugston Flores

Chynna Clugston Flores
Cover & Chapter Break Art

Guy Major
Original Cover Colorist

Steven Birch
Logo Design

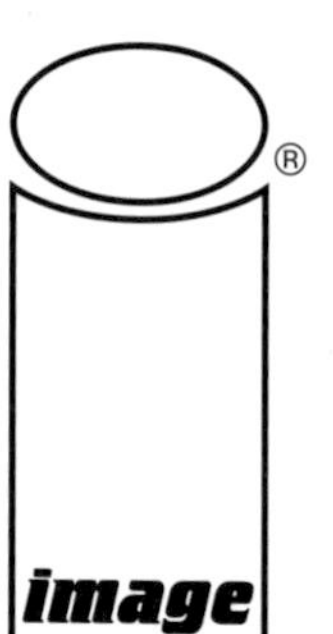

BLUE MONDAY, VOL. 2: ABSOLUTE BEGINNERS. First printing. December 2016. Published by Image Comics, Inc. Office of publication: 2001 Center Street, Sixth Floor, Berkeley, CA 94704. Contains material originally published in single magazine form as BLUE MONDAY: ABSOLUTE BEGINNERS #1-4. Printed in the USA. For information regarding the CPSIA on this printed material call: 203-595-3636 and provide reference #RICH–710950. For international rights, contact: foreignlicensing@imagecomics.com. ISBN: 978-1-63215-873-4

Chapter One
"Something About You"

SWTASS

FRIDAY, 8:33 a.m.

#THE SMITHS: "THERE IS A LIGHT THAT NEVER GOES OUT"

... TO DIE BY YOUR SIDE IS SUCH A HEAVENLY WAY TO DIIIIIIE...

BLEU!

SHIT!

SORRY. BY THE WAY, THIS IS FOR YOU. IT'S FROM PATRICK.

OH, COOL.

...

WHAT'S IN YOUR HAIR?

OH, GOD... YOU AREN'T GOING TO START WITH THE *BIRDSHIT* JOKE AGAIN, ARE YOU?

NO, I MEAN WHAT KIND OF GEL? IT, uh, SMELLS NI--

IT'S THE SAME OLD STUFF I ALWAYS USE.

WHERE HAVE *YOU* BEEN?

SCIENCE FUN!
NO, REALLY. IT'S
CREEK
GOOD! HE'S NOT PAYING ATTENTION. I'M HOME FREE.

NICE TO SEE YOU FINALLY MADE IT TO SCHOOL, FINNEGAN. YOU JUST LOOOVE DETENTION, DON'T YOU?

YOU KNOW IT'S MY HOME AWAY FROM HOME, MR. REES.

SIR REGINALD WELLINGTON
CORDIALLY INVITES YOU TO BE
HIS GUEST AT
WELLINGTON MANSION, YORKSHIRE
FOR A FORMAL DINNER
THIS SATURDAY OF OCTOBER
1936
RSVP PATRICK (209) 555-1000
PHYSICAL SCIENCE

DID YOU GUYS GET ONE OF THESE?

YEAH, PATRICK'S PARENTS ARE OUT OF TOWN THIS WEEKEND. HE WANTS US ALL TO COME OVER AND HANG OUT.
HE WANTS TO HAVE A MYSTERY PARTY LIKE SATURDAY NIGHT, SO WE'LL ALL HAVE TO DRESS UP AND STUFF. YOU KNOW, KIND OF LIKE CLUE.

CLOVER, DO YOU THINK YOU CAN HANDLE THAT? DRESSING UP?
HMPH!

WHO'S ALL GOING? IT'S KIND OF LAST MINUTE.
WELL, I KNOW ERIN IS, AND I THINK ALAN AND VICTOR ARE...
YEAH, THERE WAS WAY TOO MUCH SMIRKING GOING ON BEFORE CLASS THIS MORNING FOR THEM NOT TO BE.

GOOD GOD, WILL WE BE SAFE SLEEPING IN THE SAME HOUSE AS THOSE FREAKS?
OH, LIKE NONE OF US COULD KICK THEIR WIMPY ASSES ANYWAY. BESIDES, THEY'RE AFRAID OF CLOVER.
ARE YOU KIDDING? SHE'S THEIR FAVORITE TARGET.
Cá bhfuil tú pósta*?
SO, YOU GUYS THINK YOU CAN GO?
THAT WOULD MEAN WE HAVE TO FIND CLOTHES THAT WOULD WORK FOR THE '30s, CONVINCE OUR PARENTS THAT WE'D BE STAYING AT A SAFE PLACE, AND THEN GET A RIDE ALL THE WAY UP TO PAT'S HOUSE IN B.F.E. BY TOMORROW EVENING!
THE COSTUMES ALONE WILL TAKE FOREVER!
I DON'T HAVE ANYTHING I CAN WEAR. AND ME DA CAN'T KNOW BOYS WILL BE THERE IF WE'RE SPENDING THE NIGHT. HE'D FLIP.
BETWEEN BLEU AND ERIN'S COLLECTIONS OF COSTUMES, I'D BET MONEY YOU CAN FIND SOMETHING THAT'LL WORK. AND YOUR DAD WON'T KNOW A THING ABOUT BOYS BEING THERE. JUST SAY YOU'LL BE AT BLEU'S COUSIN'S PLACE OR SOMETHING... THAT'S PRETTY VAGUE, AND IT'S NOT TOTALLY LYING.
OKAY, GIRLS... NOW SHUT UP AND WORK!
!
BLEU, HERE'S ANOTHER DETENTION SLIP TO ADD TO THAT MOUNTAINOUS PILE I KNOW YOU'VE COLLECTED BY NOW.
Heh...
DETENTION
TARDY
*WHERE'S THE TOILET? (I'M GONNA FECKIN' PUKE.)

THAT EVENING...
#GENERAL PUBLIC: "SAVE IT FOR LATER"
GOD, CHYNNA!!!
BEAT DID "SAVE
LATER", NOT
PUBLIC!
MUSIC GURU
WHAT DID PEOPLE WEAR IN THE '30s? DID THEY EVEN HAVE CLOTHES BACK THEN? I CAN'T FIND MY LOINCLOTHS.
DON'T PLAY DUMB. YOU'RE MORONIC ENOUGH AS IT IS.
MAN, I DON'T HAVE CLOTHES THAT'LL WORK FOR ANYTHING BEFORE THE '50s.
NOTHING DRESSY ENOUGH, ANYWAY...
ME NEITHER.
WELL, WHAT DO WE DO THEN? I DON'T WANT TO LOOK LIKE A TOTAL SLOB IF THE CHICKS ARE DRESSING UP!
YEAH, YOU'RE RIGHT. I DIDN'T WANT TO HAVE TO DO THIS, BUT...
THIS? OR THIS? Hmmm... I LOOK SO GREAT IN BOTH...
TAP TAP TAP
WHAT DO YOU TWO WANT?
WE NEED HELP WITH OUR COSTUMES.
SIGH.
AS USUAL, I HAVE COME TO THE RESCUE.
WELL, IF YOU'RE GOING TO BE A SNOB ABOUT IT!

I NEED HELP, TOO!
SEE? IT'S NOT SNOBBERY, IT'S A FACT. EVERYONE KNOWS TO COME TO ME. MY HELPING YOU THREE IS A RESCUE OF SORTS. OTHERWISE, YOU'D BE STUCK IN LOUNGEWEAR FROM 1972, IF I'M NOT MISTAKEN. I BELIEVE I'LL GLOAT A LITTLE.
I DON'T SEE WHY. DO YOU HAVE THREE SUITS LYING AROUND THAT'LL FIT US ALL PERFECTLY AND BE FROM THE RIGHT ERA?
NO, I DON'T.
I REST MY CASE.
BUT I HAVE THE KEY TO THE DOOR OF THE PLAYHOUSE, WHICH ALSO HAS AN EXTENSIVE WARDROBE INSIDE.
HOW'D YOU GET THE KEY TO THAT?!
I HAVE MY WAYS.
YEAH, THE KLEPTO STRIKES AGAIN!
MEANWHILE, AT BLEU'S HOUSE...
I HAVE JUST THE THING! YOU'RE GOING TO KNOCK 'EM OUT... CLOVER THE SEDUCTRESS! HA!
WHAT ARE YOU GOING TO WEAR?
I HAVE THIS WICKED LITTLE OUTFIT. I'M GOING TO BE THE SNOTTY ENGLISH HEIRESS JUST BACK FROM SINGAPORE!
"I'M SO BORED OF TRAVELLING THE WORLD-- CAIRO ONE WEEK, ROME THE NEXT... YAWN..."
RAMONES
HOODOO GURU
OH, YES, YOU'RE SO CONTINENTAL.
GODDAMMIT, BLEU, COULDN'T I JUST WEAR A TUX?
BUZ
HELL, NO! YOU'RE GOING FEMME FATALE, BABY! THOSE GOONS WILL DROP DEAD AT THE SIGHT OF YOU!
DAMN PATRICK AND HIS STUPID THEME PARTIES.
I HAVE A FEELING THIS WEEKEND'S GOING TO GO DOWN IN HISTORY! I KNOW IT WILL! MWA HA HA HA HA!!!
IT'S JUST LIKE YOU TO THINK EVERYTHING DAVE WAKELING IS GENERAL PUBLIC.
FUCK YOU!
BOW BEFORE MY EXTENSIVE CD COLLECTION

I'M CHYNNA! "WHO'S DAVE WAKELING?!"

SHUT UP!

VICTOR, TURN OFF THE FOKIN' CAMERA BEFORE I JAM IT UP YER ARSE!
OOF, IT GETS ME ALL EXCITED WHEN YOU TALK DIRTY! WHAT ELSE ARE YOU GOING TO STICK IN MY ASS? YOUR RIDING CROP? A SLINKY?
MY FOOT IF YOU DON'T SHUT YER GOB! YOU'RE DISGUSTIN'!
KONK!
#%@$!
HEY, ALAN, CAN YOU PEEL YOUR EYES FROM BLEU'S BUM FOR TWO SECONDS? YOU MIGHT MELT IT, AND THEN WHAT'S SHE GOING TO SIT ON?
...
DON'T YOU DARE ANSWER THAT!

I TAPED SOME VIDEOS OFF OF "MUSIC EXPRESS" LAST NIGHT IF YOU GUYS WANNA WATCH 'EM... I GOT THE THOMPSON TWINS, DEPECHE MODE, AND NITZER EBB ON THERE, AND SOME OTHERS.
NICE! YEAH, LET'S GO WATCH THEM. I'M ALREADY SICK OF LOOKING AT ALAN AND VICTOR.
YE'H.
THE KINKS
ZOOM!
THUMP THUMP THUMP
WHAT ARE LENNY AND SQUIGGY UP TO?
OH, WHO CARES.
IS THIS IT? NO, THAT'S GOTTA BE PAT'S ROOM.
YOU KNOW HE HAS NO PORN AT ALL. PROBABLY JERKS OFF TO MONTGOMERY WARD'S PANTY SECTION...
HERE IT IS, THE *MASTER BEDROOM!*
LOOK AT THE SIZE OF THAT BED! IT'S LIKE A PLAYGROUND!
IS IT TOO MUCH TO ASK FOR EVERYONE TO HAVE A MIRROR ABOVE THE BED?
YEAH!

IT SHOULD BE A LAW!
NO MIRROR ABOVE YOUR BED? THAT'LL BE A $500 FINE.
LOOK, THIS IS PERFECT FOR A BIT OF THE OLD TIE-THE-WENCH-UP-AND-SLAP-SOMMA-DAT GAME.
I WONDER IF THERE'S A WAY TO LURE THE CHICKS UP HERE? WE COULD BRAINWASH 'EM...
FUMP
OKAY, THAT WOULDN'T WORK, AND WE KNOW WHY.
THEN WE COULD WRAP 'EM UP IN BITS OF CHECKERED VINYL...
DO YOU WANT TO BE ALONE?
HMM.
THE MASTER BATH...?
DIDN'T WE HEAR PAT SAY THE WENCHES SHOULD CHANGE IN HERE?
OH, MAN! WE CAN SET THE CAMERA UNDERNEATH THE BED AND FACE IT TOWARD THE BATHROOM. WE MAY LUCK OUT AND GET THEM NAKED! I HAVE HOURS OF TAPE!
WHAT WERE YOU GUYS DOING UPSTAIRS?
NOTHIN', WE WERE JUST CHECKING OUT YOUR PAD.
OKAY, JUST TRY NOT TO BREAK ANYTHING. MY PARENTS WOULD FREAK IF THEY KNEW ANYONE WAS HERE BESIDES ME.
Eww, THEY'RE BACK. LET'S GO GET READY.

ALREADY?
YEAH, PAT, YOU KNOW IT TAKES CHICKS *HOURS* TO PREPARE FOR ANYTHING.
LATER, LOSERS.

YOU KNOW WHAT WOULD BE SWEET? IF WE GOT SOME HOT LESBIAN ACTION ON FILM! DO YOU THINK THEY...?

NO, BUT IF I HAD THREE WISHES, THAT'D BE ONE OF 'EM!
HELL, THAT'D BE *ALL THREE* FOR ME!

YOU GUYS PUT THE CAMERA IN THE BEDROOM?
YEAH, FACING THE BATHROOM. WE'RE HOPING FOR NUDITY!

BLEU! CLOVER! THEY PUT THE CAMERA UNDER THE BED!
MAN!

WHAT?!

BASTARDS!

SHOOM
NOOOOOOOO!
CLOSE CALL.
BABY! YOU OKAY?
SHIT!
THAR SHE BLOWS!
LEAP!
MAN, PAT, IF THEY WOULD'A BROKE THIS, I'D HAVE MADE *YOU* PAY FOR IT!
WHAT? WHY? IT'S PROBABLY STOLEN ANYWAY. JUST STEAL A NEW ONE!
THAT'S NOT THE POINT!
WE CAN TRY AGAIN LATER. WE HAVE ALL NIGHT.
AND SO THE GUESTS DRESSED FOR THE EVENING WHILE THE ORCHESTRA ARRIVED...
IT WAS NO THIN FIVE-PIECE AFFAIR, BUT A WHOLE PIT FULL OF OBOES AND TROMBONES AND SAXOPHONES...
BACH

YOU GUYS READY YET?
KNOCK! KNOCK! KNOCK!
HELLO!
HI, PAT!
WHERE IS EVERYONE?
ARE THE GUYS READY YET?
I DON'T KNOW. MONKEYBOY GOT HERE A LITTLE WHILE AGO. I THINK ALAN AND VICTOR HAVE BEEN TRYING TO GET HIM TO SLICK BACK HIS HAIR...THERE SEEMS TO HAVE BEEN A STRUGGLE.
I GUESS MONKEYBOY WON!
SMOOTH SMOOTH SMOOTH
SEE, DON'T THEY LOOK GREAT? I GOT THEM THE CLOTHES AND TOLD THEM HOW TO DO THEIR HAIR.
CONGRATULATIONS...
MY GOD WE'RE DASHING.
INDEED.
YOU LOOK PRETTY.
THANKS...
WHAT ABOUT ME?
YOU LOOK TRAILER CHEAP. OH, SORRY-- I MEAN, TRES CHIC.
NO LUCK?
WE GOT HIS HAIR SLICKED BACK AND THEN REALIZED HE HAS NO EYES, SO WE LET HIM PUT HIS HAIR DOWN AGAIN. IT WAS JUST TOO SCARY.
THERE WAS JUST NO CONVINCING HIM, HUH?
NOPE.

HEY, GUYS!
CLOVER, DON'T YOU THINK-- WHERE'D YOU GO?
HEY, GUYS, CHECK OUT CLOVER!
COME ON, YOU LOOK SO ACE! STAND UP STRAIGHT!
DOESN'T SHE LOOK GREAT?
YOU LOOK GORGEOUS! DON'T BE SHY!
UH, T'ANKS...

WOW. EVERYONE WENT ALL OUT! THIS IS GREAT! WELL, DINNER IS READY, IF YOU ALL WANT TO GO INTO THE DINING ROOM!
LOOKING GOOD THERE, FINNEGAN.
YOU DON'T CLEAN UP SO BAD YOURSELF. IF I DIDN'T KNOW YOU OR VICTOR I'D ALMOST SAY YOU TWO WERE KINDA HOT, BUT YOUR PERSONALITIES DESTROY THAT IDEA!
OH. YOU KNOW THE THOUGHT OF ME AS YOUR MAN MAKES YOU CREAM.
DON'T FLATTER YOURSELF, ALAN. YOU AREN'T THAT BABELY!
A LOVELY DINNER!
SORRY, THE CHICKEN'S A LITTLE DRY...
EVEN IF THE CHICKEN'S A LITTLE DRY!
MAY I HAVE SOME MORE TO DRINK, PLEASE?
ME TOO AS WELL! HA HA!
YOU WANT WINE OR PUNCH?
PUNCH, ACTUALLY... IT'S REALLY TASTY!
SAME! GOOD PUNCH! PUNCH IS GOOD!
WHO SPIKED THE PUNCH?
HA HA!
YOU GUYS GOT IT TOO? OH, SHIT!
YOU MEAN ALL THREE OF YOU SPIKED IT?! IF YOU WERE GOING TO DRINK, YOU WERE ONLY SUPPOSED TO HAVE ONE GLASS OF WINE AND THAT'S IT!
IT'S SPIKED? IS THAT WHY I FEEL SO FUNNY?
LUSH.

I'M NOT A LUSH! I'VE NEVER BEEN DRUNK!
OH, YEAH? YOU CAN'T PROVE THAT. ESPECIALLY WITH THIS BEHAVIOR. I MEAN, REALLY. IT'S DISGRACEFUL. NOW, LET'S GO UPSTAIRS AND CLEAN YOU UP.
I'M NOT A LUSH! AND I'M NOT DIRTY EITHER!
Lech
OH, NO. YOU'RE DEFINITELY DIRTY. YOU NEED A GOOD LATHERING.

VICTOR, IF THAT'S YOUR FOOT ON MY LEG, I'M GOING TO CUT IT OFF WITH THIS HERE BUTTER KNIFE.
I'LL GET CLOVER SOME MORE PUNCH. SHE'S NOT HAPPY ENOUGH!
YOU GUYS ARE GETTING EVERYONE DRUNK BEFORE WE CAN EVEN PLAY THE GAME!

EVERYONE INTO THE LIVING ROOM! WE'RE STARTING THE GAME BEFORE YOU'RE ALL TOO SILLY TO FUNCTION!

THE SCENE!
THE STATELY HOME OF SIR REGINALD WELLINGTON. HIS WEEKEND GUESTS HAVE ARRIVED...
I ARRIVED IN A SWEET-ASS BENTLEY!
SHUT UP, BLEU!

SIR REGINALD'S GUESTS HAVE ARRIVED...
ONE IN PARTICULAR IN A SWEET-ASS BENTLEY, DON'T FORGET!
THE GUESTS HAVE ARRIVED AND--
HEY!
ONE IN A SWEET BENTLEY! GEEZ. CAN WE MOVE ON?!
SWEET-ASS BENTLEY. PROCEED.
THANK YOU! THE GUESTS HAVE ARRIVED AND ARE GATHERED IN THE DRAWING ROOM FOR COCKTAILS, AWAITING THEIR HOST.

AN INTRODUCTION TO THE GUESTS.

WILLIAM RUTHERFORD, SIR WELLINGTON'S ADVENTURING NEPHEW.

ELIZA MEANDERBURY, A NOVELIST

JONATHAN THOMAS, AN ARCHAEOLOGIST

ANNABETH GRAY, AN HEIRESS
SHUT UP!
WITH A SWEET-

FREDERICK STANSEL, SIR WELLINGTON'S LAWYER

ELIZABETH RIDDLE, AN ACTRESS

FRANCIS LOCKHEART, SIR WELLINGTON'S PERSONAL SECRETARY.
WHY DO I HAVE TO BE THE SECRETARY?

OKAY. SO, HERE ARE YOUR GUIDES THAT TELL YOU WHAT TO SAY AND WHAT NOT TO SAY AT WHICHEVER TIME, AND I'M SUPPOSED TO PUT IN THE TAPE NOW, SO HOLD ON. READ ONLY THE FIRST PART UNTIL IT TELLS YOU TO STOP.
OOH, ERIN, YOU WERE THE OLD BLIGHTER'S MISTRESS!
OH.
YOU AREN'T SUPPOSED TO READ THAT STUFF YET!
SO, WHO'S DEAD?
SIR WELLINGTON. AND YOU'RE ALL SUSPECTS!
DON'T TOUCH THOSE YET! THOSE ARE THE SECRET CLUES!
SMAK
WHO ARE YOU THEN?
I'M A DETECTIVE FROM SCOTLAND YARD!
I WANT TO BE MISS MONEYPENNY!
WRONG ERA AND ORGANIZATION, BLEU...
I DON'T GIVE A DAMN!!!
SHE'S A BELLIGERENT DRUNK!
FIGHT! FIGHT!
!
I TOLD YOU STAY AWAY FROM THOSE, YOU'LL SPOIL THE GAME!
AGH!
BUMP!
SPLOOSH!
OH, I'M SO SORRY, BLEU!
AW, 'S OKAY... AT LEAST I'M NOT WEARING A LIGHT COLOR. I'M GOING TO HAVE TO GO WASH THIS OUT PRETTY QUICK, THOUGH, OR IT'S GONNA REEK.

I KNOW WHO DID IT! IT WAS WILLIAM! HE'S WELLINGTON'S ILLEGITIMATE SON WHO GAMBLES TOO MUCH AND GOT WRITTEN OUT OF THE WILL IN FAVOR OF HIS TRUE HALF-SISTER, ANNABETH!
AW, MAN, YOU KILLED IT! YOU SUCK!
OH, WELL. DO YOU GUYS WANT TO CALL IT A NIGHT? I'M TOTALLY EXHAUSTED.
YEAH.
GOOD, I CAN GET THE HELL OUTTA THIS FECKIN' DRESS!
I HAD FUN, THOUGH.
IT WAS OKAY.
IS IT OKAY IF I USE YOUR PARENTS' BATH? IT'S THE ONLY ONE THAT DOESN'T HAVE A WINDOW WITH A LITTLE HILL IN FRONT OF IT WHERE I CAN BE HARASSED BY THE DIPSHITS.
SURE.
!
VROOM!
WHY THE HELL ARE THEY LAUGHING? I KNOW THEY CAN'T SEE ME FROM THE GROUND...
HA! HA! HA! HA!
HEY! SHUT UP! YOU CAN'T SEE ME FROM THERE, SO DON'T EVEN PLAY THAT!

THEY AREN'T GOING TO SCARE ME! AND I'M NOT GOING TO SMELL LIKE WINE ALL NIGHT!
IF I JUST MAKE SURE I DON'T GET TOO CLOSE TO THE WINDOW, THEY DEFINITELY CAN'T SEE ME... I WISH THIS THING HAD BLINDS!

GUYS! COME BACK IN HERE! WHAT ARE YOU DOING?

HA! HA! HA!
SHUT UP! I KNOW YOU CAN'T SEE ME!
#THOMPSON TWINS: "COME INSIDE"

MY GOD, SHE REALLY HAS NO IDEA WE'RE RIGHT HERE! SHE THINKS WE'RE ON THE GROUND!
OH, MAN, THIS IS TOO PERFECT!
HA HA HA!!!

I GUESS WE'RE GOING TO FIND OUT IF HER HAIR IS NATURALLY BLUE OR NOT!

OH, MY GOD...
YES!!!
BAM!

WHAT THE FUCK?
STOOPID!

FUCK!!
WE MISSED IT!!!
HA HA! HOH GAAD!

WHAT IS SHE DOING?

OH, SHE'S TRYING TO SLIDE INTO THE TUB SO WE DON'T SEE HER! TOO LATE, BLEU! HA-HA!
#%@$!

OH, MAN, SHE'S SOAPING HERSELF UP! THAT SHOULD BE MY JOB!
YOU THINK SHE'D LET ME IN AND SHAVE HER LEGS IF I ASKED REALLY NICELY?

YOU? NO WAY... NOW IF I ASKED...

YOU WISH! ALL THE BITCHES WANT ME.
HA-HA! YOU'RE SO ON DOPE.

WHAT THE HELL'S WRONG WITH ME LATELY? CAN'T GET MY MIND OFF OF THAT DUMB CHICK.
OH, MAN... I COULDN'T BE... NAH, NOT WITH BLEU.
NO WAY.
YOU THINK?
#SAPPHIRES: "GOTTA HAVE YOUR LOVE"
NAH.
NO, I DON'T CARE WHAT SHE THINKS.
CLASSIFIED
FOR SALE
SCOOTERS & MOPEDS
BUT IT'S JUST FLIRTING!
MOD FASHION FILE
THAT DOES IT!
DOES WHAT?
IT'S FINAL. I'M GOING TO ASK BLEU OUT!

LIKE, ON A DATE? ARE YOU SURE?
YEAH, WHAT'S WRONG WITH THAT?
GLARE
NOTHING, JUST...
JUST WHAT?
DO YOU REALLY THINK SHE'LL GO OUT WITH YOU? I MEAN, I THOUGHT SHE ONLY LIKED THIRTYSOMETHINGS?
OH, THE MR. BISHOP THING? THAT'S GOTTA BE JUST A PASSING PHASE.
SHE'LL WISE UP WHEN SOMEONE HER OWN AGE ACTUALLY ASKS HER OUT.
GET OUT OF THE GARAGE! YOU GUYS SHOULD BE ASHAMED OF YOURSELVES!
IS MONKEYBOY STILL ALIVE?
#ZZZ#
HEY! WE GOT HER ON TAPE, MAN!
SHUT UP! REALLY?
HA! HA! HA! HA!
SLAM!
OH, MY GOD?!! OH, MY GOD!!!
NO WAY!
HOP!
YOU FUCKERS SHUT UP! YOU COULDN'T SEE ME FROM THE GROUND! CLOVERRR!

BLEU, YOU AREN'T GOING TO BE HAPPY ABOUT THIS, BUT I THINK THEY DID GET YOU ON VIDEO! I CAN'T GET IN, THE DOOR IS LOCKED TO PAT'S ROOM.
WHAT!?! HOW???
DIDN'T YOU SEE THE GARAGE ACROSS THE WAY? THERE'S A WINDOW RIGHT ACROSS FROM THE BATHROOM.
AAH!
THAT'S FUCKED UP!
BAM! BAM! BAM!
YOU BASTARDS BETTER FUCKING ERASE WHATEVER YOU GOT ON THAT TAPE!!!
I CAN'T BELIEVE YOU!!! HOW COULD YOU DO SOMETHING SO HORRIBLE TO ME?!
OKAY, OKAY! WE'RE ERASING IT! GEEZ, WE COULDN'T SEE ANYTHING ANYWAY! (SNORT)
YEAH, BLEU. OF COURSE THERE'S NO WAY WE'D REALLY KEEP IT AND PASS IT AROUND. I MEAN, WE'RE YOUR FRIENDS, RIGHT?
SOME FRIENDS!!! YOU BETTER PROMISE ME YOU ERASED IT!!!
WE PROMISE.
YOU PRICKS BETTER PROVE IT'S ERASED, TOO!
GO GET INTO YOUR BEDCLOTHES, BLEU. I'LL CHECK THE TAPE AND SEE.
I WON'T KILL THEM IF THEY DESTROY IT. I'LL JUST MUTILATE THEM A LITTLE!!!
FUCKERS!

SLAM!
DID YOU PRICKS REALLY ERASE IT?
OF COURSE WE DID!
COME ON, BLEU, IT WASN'T ON THE TAPE. ALL'S SAFE NOW.
WELL, BUT THEY'VE SEEN ME NAKED! HOW COULD I EVER LIVE THAT DOWN?
I'M SURE NO ONE WILL KNOW ABOUT IT... I MEAN, IT COULD HAVE BEEN WORSE. IT'S NOT LIKE THEY FILMED YOU CRAPPING OR ANYTHING!
BESIDES, IT'S GONE...
SHOE GAZA
... WHAT HARM CAN IT DO NOW?
EVEN IF THE DORKS SAID SOMETHING, HOW RELIABLE DO YOU THINK THE SCHOOL SEES THEM?
YEAH...
SHOE GAZA
THAT MONDAY...
SORRY, MR. REES...
IT'S YOUR DETENTION, KID.
WHAT'S WRONG, GUYS?
BLEU, I HAVE SOME GOOD NEWS AND SOME BAD NEWS.
THE GOOD NEWS IS YOU WERE ACTUALLY RIGHT ABOUT SOMETHING.
WHAT'S THAT?
THE WEEKEND DID GO DOWN IN HISTORY.
I THINK YOU CAN FIGURE OUT THE BAD NEWS...
THUMP
BLEU?

Chapter Two
"Favourite Shirts"
CCMTV

THE CRAMPS
"BIKINI GIRLS WITH MACHINE GUNS"

SIGH

EFFERSON HIGH
L'S VOLLYBALL THURS 5:30
GER FOOTBALL VS. SIERRA
FRIDAY 8 PM
BLEU BUTT NAKED
GO BIG BLUE!
HUH?
THAT DOESN'T MAKE ANY SENSE, I'M FULLY--
-- EXPOSED!
SHIT!!!
AAAGH!
HOW THE HELL DID I GET OUT OF THE HOUSE LIKE THIS??
THIS IS WORSE THAN WEARING HOT PANTS AND FISHNETS... AND NO ONE SAID ANYTHING?!?
HA HA HA
HA HA HA!
STOP IT RIGHT THERE, FINNEGAN! NOT ONLY ARE YOU RUNNING, BUT YOU KNOW VERY WELL WE DON'T TOLERATE NAKEDNESS AT JEFFERSON HIGH WITHOUT A HALL PASS!
B-BUT I'M WEARING SOCKS AND SHOES! SHOULDN'T THAT COUNT FOR SOMETHING?
TO THE OFFICE WITH YOU!
GET MOVING!
AW, Come on.
PRINCIPA
BRR...

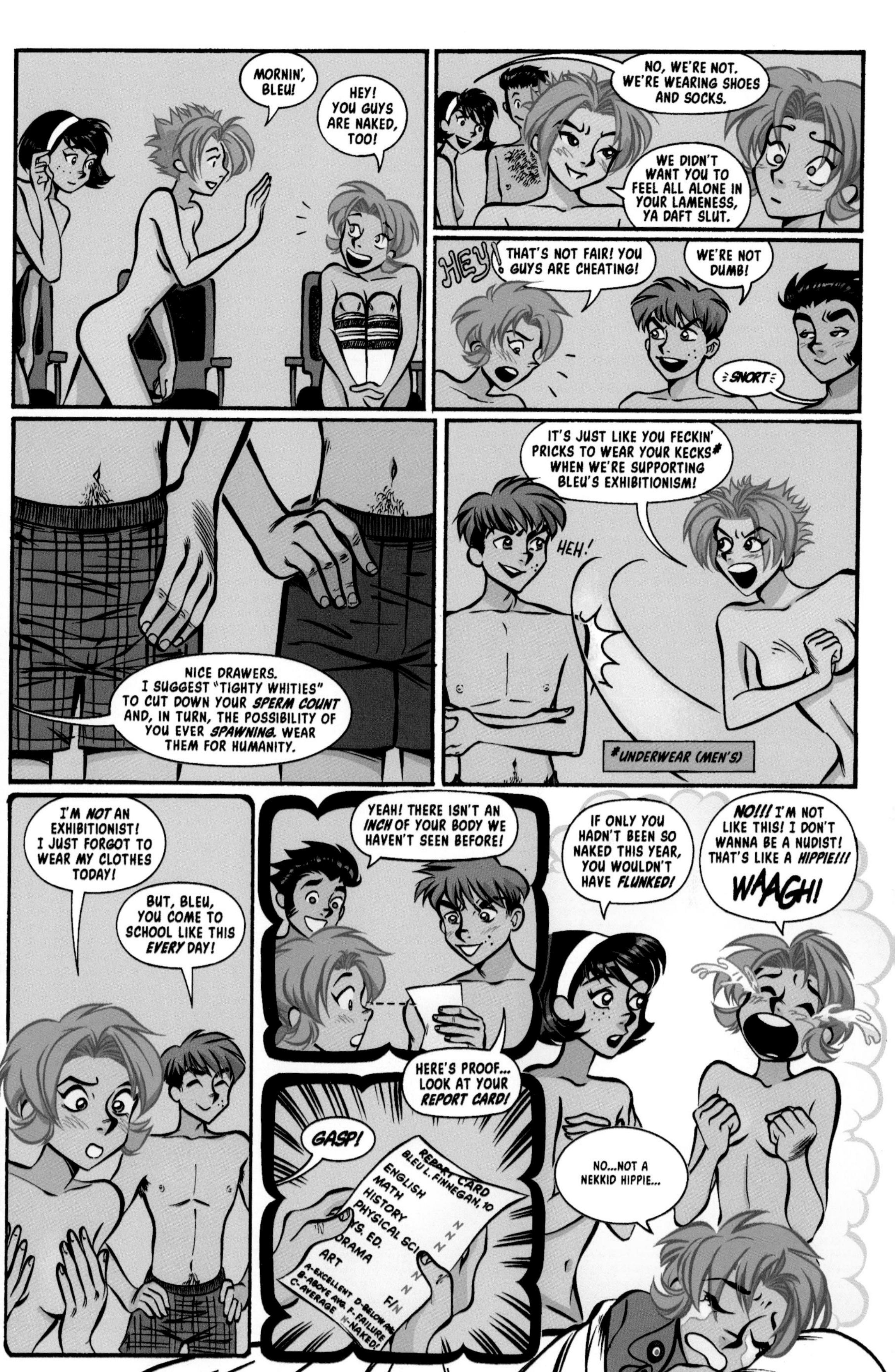
MORNIN', BLEU!
HEY! YOU GUYS ARE NAKED, TOO!
NO, WE'RE NOT. WE'RE WEARING SHOES AND SOCKS.
WE DIDN'T WANT YOU TO FEEL ALL ALONE IN YOUR LAMENESS, YA DAFT SLUT.
HEY!
THAT'S NOT FAIR! YOU GUYS ARE CHEATING!
WE'RE NOT DUMB!
SNORT
NICE DRAWERS. I SUGGEST "TIGHTY WHITIES" TO CUT DOWN YOUR SPERM COUNT AND, IN TURN, THE POSSIBILITY OF YOU EVER SPAWNING. WEAR THEM FOR HUMANITY.
IT'S JUST LIKE YOU FECKIN' PRICKS TO WEAR YOUR KECKS# WHEN WE'RE SUPPORTING BLEU'S EXHIBITIONISM!
HEH!
#UNDERWEAR (MEN'S)
I'M NOT AN EXHIBITIONIST! I JUST FORGOT TO WEAR MY CLOTHES TODAY!
BUT, BLEU, YOU COME TO SCHOOL LIKE THIS EVERY DAY!
YEAH! THERE ISN'T AN INCH OF YOUR BODY WE HAVEN'T SEEN BEFORE!
HERE'S PROOF... LOOK AT YOUR REPORT CARD!
GASP!
REPORT CARD
BLEU L. FINNEGAN, 10
ENGLISH N
MATH N
HISTORY N
PHYSICAL SCI N
PHYS. ED. N
DRAMA N
ART F/N
A-EXCELLENT D-BELOW AVG.
B-ABOVE AVG. F-FAILURE
C-AVERAGE N-NAKED!
IF ONLY YOU HADN'T BEEN SO NAKED THIS YEAR, YOU WOULDN'T HAVE FLUNKED!
NO!!! I'M NOT LIKE THIS! I DON'T WANNA BE A NUDIST! THAT'S LIKE A HIPPIE!!!
WAAGH!
NO...NOT A NEKKID HIPPIE...

WAKE UP, BLEU.
WOULD SOMEONE PASS ME THAT MOOSE SKIN PLEASE, I CAN'T FEEL MY CHEEKS--
BLEU, IT'S OKAY, YOU'RE FULLY DRESSED. YOU SHOULD GO GET SOMETHING TO EAT SINCE LUNCHTIME JUST STARTED, RIGHT?
SNORF
UH? OKAY...
JHS
HAHAHAHAHA!
NURSE
WELL, THAT TAKES CARE OF THEIR MASTURBATION MATERIAL FOR A WEEK!
BIG DEAL, SHE ONLY SHAVED HER LEGS! I WOULD HAVE PUT ON A REAL SHOW!
DUDE, THAT'S FUCKED UP! CAN YOU IMAGINE THEM ALL HUNCHED OVER THE TOILET SPANKING AWAY TO YOU?
GROSS!
mope
mope
mope
BWAHAHA
HAHAHAW

HOY, BLEU, HOW WAS THE NURSE'S OFFICE? IS IT MALIGNANT?
GREAT. I'M FINE. I LOVE PASSING OUT IN FRONT OF TWENTY PEOPLE THAT HATE ME.
TWENTY-TWO. REMEMBER, RISSA AND I HATE YOU, TOO.
TWENTY-TWO, THEN.
I DON'T KNOW WHAT YOU'RE SO UPSET ABOUT. YOU SHOULDN'T MAKE SUCH A FEDERAL CASE OUT OF IT. MOST OF THOSE PEOPLE DIDN'T LIKE YOU IN THE FIRST PLACE.
OH, YEAH? MAYBE I DON'T LIKE BEING THOUGHT OF AS SOME KIND OF STREAKING ORGY-MONGER!
MAYBE UNLIKE SOME PEOPLE NAMED ERIN, I KNOW WHAT MODESTY IS!
ANYWAY, BLEU, I HAVE AN IDEA ABOUT DOING SOMETHING THAT COULD AT LEAST GIVE YOU A BIT OF COMFORT IN YOUR TIME OF DARKNESS.
WHAT'S HER PROBLEM?
YEAH, WE WERE TALKING ABOUT THIS AFTER YOU WERE CARRIED OUT OF SCIENCE...
IT WAS FUNNY, YOU WERE COMPLETELY DROOLING ON YOURSELF AND--
FUCK!
JAB
--SO WE DECIDED TO CHALLENGE THE PRICKS TO A MATCH.
A SOCCER GAME??
AND NOT JUST ANY FOOTBALL MATCH... IT'S GOT A DIFFERENT SET OF RULES.
HOOLIGAN RULES!

I ALREADY TALKED TO MY DAD ABOUT LETTING US USE THE SOCCER FIELD TONIGHT. HE SAID YES, AS LONG AS NO ONE KNOWS HE WAS THERE.*
YOU BE THE GOALIE, AND WE'LL DO THE REST! YOU CAN JUST SIT BACK AND ENJOY THE SHOW!
* RISSA'S DAD IS THE ASSISTANT PRINCIPAL AT JEFFERSON HIGH.

WAIT A SECOND, THOUGH... THEY KNOW HOW GOOD CLOVER IS AT SOCCER. THEY'LL NEVER ACCEPT A CHALLENGE!

OH, YES, THEY *WILL*... IF WE CHALLENGE THEM IN FRONT OF *EVERYONE*. THEY WON'T BACK DOWN AND LOOK LIKE WIMPS. THEY'D SOONER SHAG LABELLEPHANT.
I HOPE SO. I GUESS WE'LL SEE, RIGHT?

AND SO...
A *WHAT?* AGAINST *YOU THREE?*
HOLD ON A MINUTE.

DUDE, EVERYONE'S STARING AT US.
I KNOW! WE CAN'T LOOK STUPID, WE GOTTA ACCEPT.
THEY SAID THEY'D HAVE A REF THERE AND EVERYTHING.
TRUE, AND IT'S JUST GOING TO BE US AND THEM, LOSER BUYS PIZZA.
I'M IN THE MOOD FOR SOME FREE PIZZA. LET'S DO IT.

NO PROBLEM.
TONIGHT AT 7:00.

LIKE CLOCKWORK!

Ahem. SO, BLEU...
DON'T TALK TO ME!
Aw, WHAT'S *WRONG*, BLEU? ARE YOU STILL *SORE* ABOUT SOMETHING? DON'T WORRY. I BET MR. BISHOP DOESN'T KNOW ANYTHING ABOUT HIS STAR STUDENT'S WET 'N' SOAPY *SEXCAPADES* LAST WEEKEND.
"OH, MR. BISHOP! I'D NEVER LET THREE BOYS VIDEOTAPE ME WHILE I SHAVE ALL MY BODY HAIR OFF AND DISCOVER NEW USES FOR SHOWER HEADS!"
ARG!
SMA

OW!
C'MON, BLEU. LET'S GET SOME EATS.
BLEU, MY LOVE! I DON'T CARE ABOUT TEACHING ANYMORE! I JUST WANT TO LIVE FOR YOU, MA CHERIE!
OH, REALLY!
YOU DUMB BOYS HEAR THAT?
#SIGH#
MR. BISHOP...
WELL, ACTUALLY, THAT USED TO BE TRUE... UNTIL I LEARNED OF YOUR LITTLE ILLICIT VIDEO.
GASP
BWAHAHA!
YOU SUCK. GO AWAY.
OH, GOD! HE MUST HAVE HEARD ALL KINDS OF HORRIBLE THINGS! CLOVER, DO YOU THINK HE KNOWS?
WHO CARES?
GLARE
#SIGH#
OF COURSE NOT. YOU KNOW TEACHERS DON'T LISTEN TO STUDENTS' GOSSIP. THEY'RE ABOVE THAT CHILDISH STUFF.
THERE'S THAT FINNEGAN KID.
I HEARD THE STUDENTS TALKING ABOUT SOME VIDEO WITH HER NAKED ON IT THAT'S BEING PASSED AROUND SCHOOL. HOW SCARY IS THAT?

I HEARD THAT TODAY, TOO! WE SHOULD SEE IF WE CAN GET HER THROWN OUT, YOU KNOW. I BET IT WAS SOME KIND OF AMATEUR PORN, OR SOMETHING LIKE THAT... YOU KNOW THOSE ADDICTS SHE HANGS AROUND.
SHE MAKES THE GOOD STUDENTS AT THIS SCHOOL LOOK BAD.
NO, NO. SHE WAS TAPED BATHING. NOTHING ELSE.
WHAT'S ALL THIS?
← RIGHTWING PIGEONS!
UNFORTUNATELY, SOME OF HER "FRIENDS" TAPED HER BATHING AS A JOKE, AND NOW THE WHOLE SCHOOL KNOWS ABOUT IT.
BUT SHE WAS UNAWARE THIS WAS HAPPENING AT THE TIME, RIGHT?
I'M SURE SHE WAS.
I THINK YOU MAY BE TOO HARSH ON HER, MIKE. I WOULDN'T LET MY DAUGHTER HANG OUT WITH HER IF I THOUGHT SHE WAS BAD.
I DON'T KNOW... SHE'S PRETTY DAMN WEIRD. GIRLS LIKE THAT ARE ALWAYS PROMISCUOUS.
BACK AT THE TREE...
I'M GOING TO ASK RIGHT NOW. CHECK IT OUT.
GLARMF
HEY, BLEU--
BLEU!
SHHM!
PINEAPPLE!!!
WHAT?
HOW TO ROAST ARMADILLO
BOP!

YARM
WHY ARE YOU EATING SO FAST?
WE STILL HAVE SOME TIME LEFT.
WHO ARE YOU CALLIN' CRAZY?!
OH CHRIST, BLEU. GIVE IT UP.
glug glug glug
WHAT'S SHE UP TO NOW?
SHE'S GOT IT DOWN TO THE MINUTE.
SHE KNOWS PRECISELY THE TIME HE HEADS BACK TO HIS CLASS, AND WHAT ROUTE HE TAKES.
YOU DON'T MEAN...?
SHE EVEN KNOWS THE TYPICAL DAYS HE TAKES A SLIGHTLY DIFFERENT ROUTE.
SHE'S GOT A LITTLE JOURNAL ON HIM, THAT'S HOW BAD IT IS.
DOES SHE TALK TO HIM EVERY TIME?
OH, NO. MOSTLY SHE JUST WATCHES HIM.
THAT'S NOT HEALTHY.
I TELL HER THAT. IT'S NOT LIKE SHE'S *PSYCHO*, BUT SHE'S COMPLETELY DISTRACTED BY HIM.
THERE'S NO WAY THAT IT WILL EVER TURN INTO ANYTHING.
SHE'S JUST ASKING FOR ANOTHER LETDOWN.

STUDENT STORE
I DON'T SEE HIM ANYWHERE. HOW DID I MISS HIM?

HELLO, BLEU.
!!!

OH, HI!

YOU ON YOUR WAY TO CLASS?
...

DUH!

SO... HOW IS EVERYTHING LATELY?
UH, OKAY... I GUESS...
PLEASE DON'T LET HIM KNOW, PLEASE DON'T LET HIM KNOW!

THERE'S SOME CRAZY RUMORS FLOATING AROUND SCHOOL ABOUT YOU.

IT'S NOT WHAT YOU THINK! I'M NOT LIKE THAT! STUPID BOYS, I HATE THEM ! I HATE ALL OF THEM! IT'S THEIR FAULT, I DIDN'T KNOW AND CLOVER SAID, BUT THEY LIED AND...!!! GOD!!!

?

PROMISCUOUS MY FOOT. THAT KID WOULD KEEL OVER IF A BOY EVEN WINKED AT HER.
GOOD. LAST OF A DYING BREED.

THAT NIGHT...
GOOD JOB ON ASKING BLEU OUT, DUDE.
FUCK OFF. SHE WAS COMPLETELY HYSTERICAL TODAY.
MAN, SHE'S LIKE THAT ALL THE TIME. WHY BOTHER?
SHUT THE HELL UP! I'LL ASK HER TONIGHT. SHE WAS JUST OUT OF IT EARLIER, CAUSE SHE PASSED OUT AT SCHOOL AND EVERYTHING.

SHE'LL BE BESIDE HERSELF AFTER I TALK TO HER... AND SHE'LL TOSS THE IDEA ABOUT DATING THAT DORKY TEACHER OF HERS TO THE WIND.
SURE SHE WILL.

YOU'LL SEE. HOW LONG HAS IT BEEN SINCE A REAL GUY HAS ASKED HER OUT?
I'VE NEVER SEEN IT HAPPEN.
DUNNO.

DID YOU FIND SOMEONE ELSE TO MAKE THREE ON THE TEAM?
MONKEYBOY WAS THE ONLY ONE WHO WANTED TO GET ANYWHERE NEAR THE FIELD. I'M NOT WORRIED... IF WE HAVE A REF, CLOVER HAS TO PLAY BY THE RULES, AND THAT MEANS WE'LL TOTALLY BEAT THEM.
I DON'T THINK SHE CAN WIN AT SOCCER WITHOUT KNOCKING PEOPLE OUT.
SHOE!
MODESTY BLAISE
NYC

WIN OR LOSE, AT LEAST WE GET TO WATCH HER JIGGLE ALL OVER THE FIELD. I'D LOSE AN EYEBALL OR SOMETHING FOR THAT!
LET'S GO!

JHS SOCCER FIELD, 7:03 P.M.
PEANUTS!!!
PEANUTS...?
THEY'RE SCARED! THEY'RE NOT GOING TO SHOW!
AREN'T YOU SUPPOSED TO BE ON THE FIELD?
NAH, I'M JUST HERE TO REPAIR THE GUYS AT HALF-TIME. I BROUGHT THE FIRST AID KIT.
PO'NUTS
DINGO BOINGO
DORK
HOOLIGAN
Ahh.
?
WHAT'S THAT?
OMIGOD, YOU GUYS! I JUST HEARD THE WORST THING!
SHOULD HAVE KNOWN, BUT... DIM JUST SLIPPED AND TOLD ME THAT THE TAPE REALLY WASN'T ERASED, AND SOME OTHERS HAVE ACTUALLY SEEN IT...!
WOT?!
FUCK!!!
DO YOU THINK THAT'S TRUE?!
THOSE LYIN' BASTARDS!
I WOULDN'T PUT IT PAST THEM, THEY'RE ALWAYS FULLA SHIT.
BOYS...
GRRR
... PREPARE FOR MUTILATION.
HOOLIGAN

IT'S JUST GONNA BE *US*, HUH?!
SHIT!

HA!
NO WAY. WE'RE OUTTA HERE.

HOY! LOOK! THEY ACTUALLY *SHOWED UP!* WHY DON'T YOU COME *JOIN US*, BOYS?
HOOLIG

Aw, HELL.
WELL, AT LEAST WE STILL HAVE A *REF*, RIGHT?

NO FUCKING WAY. ISN'T THAT *TRAVIS?*
DIDN'T YOU ASK ANYTHING AT ALL ABOUT HAVING A *LEGITIMATE REFEREE?!*

Heh.

GOD! WHAT DID WE GET OURSELVES INTO?!
THIS ISN'T FAIR!
ALL RIGHT, I TRUST EVERYONE'S READY?
YOU MADE IT!
NO POSITIONS. MY WORD IS FINAL. IF YOU HAVE A PROBLEM WITH MY DECISIONS, YOU CAN TALK TO ME ABOUT IT... BUT DON'T EXPECT TO LEAVE WITHOUT A LIMP IF YOU DO.
NOW, LET'S FIGURE OUT WHO TAKES WHAT SIDE. YOU CALL IT, VICTOR.
HEADS.
HEADS IT IS. LADIES KICK OFF.
LIKE IT MATTERS WOT SIDE YA TAKE. GOOD LUCK... YOU'LL NEED IT!
I GUESS WE'LL TAKE THAT SIDE...
BAP!
HOOLIGAN
WHAT THE--?! DID YOU WEAR BIKING SHOES?!
JESUS... GO GET IN THE GOAL BOX, THEN!
I DON'T HAVE ANY CLEATS!
THE SMITHS
huff
huff
KLIK

SOMEONE HELP! HEY!
AAAGH!
KILL 'UM!
TICK TICK
TICK TICK
HOY!!! YA PRICKS PREPARED TO MEET TH' ALMIGHTY?!!
TICK TICK
TICK TICK
TICK TICK
SOMEBODY HELP! ANYBODY?!?
TWEEEEE
KICKOFF!

#SUPERGRASS
"CHEAPSKATE"

IF YOU THINK WE'RE JUST GOING TO LET YOU WIN, YOU'RE PRETTY STUPID!
DUDE, DON'T ENCOURAGE HER! ARE YOU CRAZY?!
Oh, really!

Heh-heh. JUST TRY TO GET THE BALL FROM ME, YA TWAT.
THAT'LL BE...

... EASY?!
Hey! 'MEMBER THAT TIME CLOVER KICKED ALAN IN THE NOGS? THAT WAS MY FAVORITE!

HAHAHA!
OOOH! DAAANG!!!
CH-CHEAP SHOT!

DIDN'T YOU SEE THAT!? WHERE'S HER YELLOW CARD, HUH?
THAT WAS SUCH A FOUL! COME ON, YOU KNOW SHE SHARPENS THOSE THINGS!!!
I SAW NO FOUL, MATE.
IDIOT! GO DEFEND!

GOOOAAALL!

WHAT?!

OKAY, LET'S TRY THAT AGAIN. WE WERE JUST WARMING UP.
SURE.
EMPIRE
GRRRRR...
EMPIRE
HEY, THE BALL IS OVER TH--
GYAAAAARR!
OOF!
KRAK
HAHA!
BAM!
GOOOAAALL!
OLIGAN
YOU KNOW WHAT? WE'RE JUST GONNA GO AHEAD AND KICK OFF FOR YA NOW.
IT'S NOT LIKE YOU'LL KEEP THE BALL, ANYWAY.
VICTOR, WE'RE GOING TO HAVE TO DO ANYTHING WE CAN TO GET THE BALL AWAY FROM THAT BANSHEE!
WE GOTTA REMEMBER, SHE'S JUST A CHICK.
YEAH...
AIN'T NO WOMAN GONNA TAKE US DOWN!!!
LET'S GO KICK SOME GIRLIE ASS LIKE REAL MEN!
YEAH!

CHARGE!!!
COME AAAHN!!!
HOOLIGAN
TAP
BOOM!
YA FECKERS!!
OH, THAT HAD TO HURT. BOOT TO THE HEAD!
THOUGHT THEY WOULD'VE GIVEN UP BY NOW!
THEY MUST BE PRETTY STUPID TO STAY IN THIS LONG... OR MASOCHISTIC!
OW, FUCK!
GOOAALL!
WHATEVER HAPPENED TO THEIR GOAL-KEEPER?
I THINK THAT'S HIM OVER THERE, STANDING AROUND LIKE AN IDIOT!
I WAS WONDERIN' WHO THAT WAS. I THOUGHT HE WAS FROM SPECIAL ED, THE WAY HE'S BEEN CARRYIN' ON.
HA HA HA
WOULD SOMEONE PLEASE HELP ME OFF THIS THING?
DUDE, WE CAN'T LET THEM BEAT US 800 TO NOTHING! WE GOTTA GET AT LEAST ONE GOAL, FOR GOD'S SAKE!
I KNOW!
I HAVE AN IDEA!
OKAY, AFTER THIS RESTART, I'LL TACKLE CLOVER AND HOLD HER DOWN.
YOU JUST HAVE TO STEAL THE BALL AND MAKE A GOAL! I KNOW WE CAN DO THAT MUCH!
YEAH! OKAY!

GO!
WHA--?
Uh-oh! HE GOT HER!
er... KIND OF.
HA!
I GOT HER! I GOT HER!
FECK AFF!
I CAN'T GET THE BALL, MAN!
SHIT!
GET THE FECK AFF!
I GOT HER!
VICTOR! HURRY UP!! GET THE GODDAMN BALL!
RRRIP!
...
...
...
OH, SHIT.

WHAT ARE YOU...

... LOOKIN' AT?!?!
KRAK!

THEY'RE HUGE!

SHUT UP! THAT'S YOUR SISTER!
WISH SHE WAS MY SISTER!
BOP

SHUT UP! THA'S MY SISTER!
SMAK

HOLY SHIT, DUDE!
I THINK SHE ACTUALLY SPROUTED HORNS! WHAT'S SHE DOING?
LOOK AT ALAN GO!
DAMN, RISSA. YOU SHOULD TALK TO YOUR DAD ABOUT GETTING THEM TO DO THAT EVERY FRIDAY. THE SCHOOL COULD SAVE HUNDREDS ON LAWN CARE!

HALF-TIME!
BOYS, GO SORT OUT THAT DAFT GOALIE OF THEIRS.

YOU STUCK OR SOMETHIN'?
OH, THANK YOU! CAN YOU HELP ME GET OFF THIS THING??

WHY DON'T YOU JUST UNTIE YOUR SHOE?
THE LACE IS IN A KNOT AND IT'S TOO TIGHT TO GET MY FOOT OUT...
ARE THOSE BIKING SHOES? YOU DON'T EVEN HAVE PROPER BOOTS?
THE SMITHS

LET'S TRY TO GET HIM OFF THIS THING, RIGHT?
OWWW GAD!!!

sob
SORRY, YOU'RE STUCK!
YOU'RE GONNA HAF'TA LIVE HERE NOW!

UHNNNN...
OH, WHAT THE HELL'S THIS?
I THINK THAT USED TO BE ALAN!
EMPIRE

WHAT THE FUCK DO YOU WANT? YOU LOOK LIKE SHIT!
≥SNORF≤ I TRIED TALKING TO YOU EARLIER-- YOU WANNA GO OUT WITH ME SOMETIME...
A LITTLE DINNER, A LITTLE DANCIN'...
HA! HA! HA!
I KNOW YOU MUST BE OVERJOYED THAT I ASKED YOU AND ALL ≥WHEEZE≤ BUT DON'T CRY OR ANYTHING. YOU CAN, heh-heh, THANK ME LATER.
BLEU?
I CAN'T BELIEVE YOU!
WHAT?
FIRST YOU LIE TO ME ABOUT ERASING THE VIDEO, THEN YOU TALK ABOUT IT ALL OVER SCHOOL, MAYBE EVEN SHOWED IT AROUND ALREADY!
AND THEN YOU HAVE THE NERVE TO MAKE FUN OF ME LIKE THIS?!?
BUT I'M SERIOUS! I WANNA TAKE YOU OUT!
GYAAAARR!
MY NODE!!
@#%*&!
SO, NOW'S NOT THE RIGHT TIME?
ARRAGH!
YEESH!
COME ON, I'LL CLEAN YOU UP!
JESUS, I WAS JUST TRYING TO ASK HER OUT, THEN SHE HAS TO GO ALL CRAZY ON ME!
Y-YOU ASKED HER OUT?
YEAH, BUT SHE THINKS I'M JOKING! AND I GUESS SHE'S ACTUALLY MAD ABOUT THE WHOLE VIDEO THING.
I DON'T SEE WHY.
WELL, I'D GO OUT WITH YOU...
ANY TIME.
NO THANKS. I LIKE GIRLS WITH A LITTLE CLASS.

BURRP!

HA-HA! GOOD ONE, DUDE!

Hmm...

UUURGH...

glug glug glug

GRR...

WELL, IF YOU WANT TO CONVINCE BLEU TO GO OUT WITH YOU, YOU'RE GOING TO HAVE TO PROVE TO HER YOU'RE SERIOUS.

SNORF FIGURE THAT ONE OUT ALL ON YOUR OWN? I JUST NEED TO KNOW *HOW.*

TRY THE USUAL.

FLOWERS, PRESENTS... TELL HER HOW YOU FEEL, LIKE IN A LETTER, OR ON A TAPE...

YOU KNOW, SWEEP HER OFF HER FEET.

YOU THINK SHE'D LIKE THAT STUFF?

EVERY GIRL LIKES THAT. *THINK PINK.*

HEH HEH.

I CAN DO THAT.

HI, VICTOR. WHERE'S IT HURT?

GUH. EVERYWHERE.

♪ MONKEY MONKEY MONKEY MONKEY, MONKEY! ♫

I THINK BLEU'S THE BEST CHOICE FOR YOU.
BUT I *REALLY* LIKE CLOVER...

I HATE TO TELL YOU THIS, BUT... I DON'T THINK CLOVER'S REALLY *INTO BOYS.* FORGET ABOUT IT.
GO FOR BLEU. YOU TWO WERE *MADE* FOR EACH OTHER. I *KNOW* SHE LIKES YOU. YOU JUST HAVE TO SHOW INTEREST.
CLOVER'S A... ? A...?
BUT, I THOUGHT SHE WAS A *CATHOLIC?*
YEAH. *SOME CATHOLIC.* ANYWAY, LIKE I SAID... BLEU'S THE TICKET.
WHAT DO I *DO?* ALAN'S GOING TO ASK HER OUT!
YOU HAVE TO TELL HER HOW YOU FEEL.

I CAN'T DO THAT... I'D FEEL TOO STUPID! WHAT IF SHE DIDN'T LIKE ME AFTER ALL?
THEN YOU'RE GOING TO HAVE TO KEEP ALAN FROM DATING HER, BECAUSE SHE'LL PROBABLY END UP GOING OUT WITH HIM IF YOU DON'T DO SOMETHING!
I MEAN, SHE'S GOT TO GO OUT WITH *SOMEONE,* DOESN'T SHE?

YOU JUST HAVE TO KEEP THEM FROM DATING UNTIL YOU GROW ENOUGH SPINE TO ASK HER OUT FOR YOURSELF.
YOU CAN DO IT.
I GUESS.
TIME FOR YOUR *RESTART!* YOU BASTARDS *READY??*
YEAHHH...

TICK
TICK
TICK
TICK
TICK

TWEEEEE!!!
HAHA!
THUD!
THWAP!
!

WOO! THAT WAS THE BEST SOCCER GAME I'VE EVER SEEN!
SHORTEST ONE, TOO!
SOMEONE! YIIII!!!
THE SMITHS

HI, MR. MEADE! THANKS FOR LETTING US USE THE FIELD!
YEAH, THANKS, DAD!
SURE. REMEMBER, I WAS NEVER HERE TONIGHT!

THIS IS GOING TO BE THE BEST TASTING PIZZA EVER! I HOPE THE CHEAP BASTARDS BROUGHT MONEY!
GUYS?
HELLO? Aw, MAN!

K-CHHKKK!
NO!
THE SMITHS
SHIKSHIKSHIKSHIKSHIKSHIKSHIKSHIK

No!

sniff-sniff
snuffle

Chapter Three
"To Sir, With Love"

ALAN'S HARMONIOUS HOME, 7:00 AM.
ALAAAN! GET UP NOW!
SHUT UP, COW!!!
ALAN, LEAVE YOUR SISTER ALONE! APOLOGIZE TO HER FOR CALLING HER A HEIFER! AND MAKE ME SOME EGGS!
I CALL 'EM LIKE I SEE 'EM! AND MAKE THEM YOURSELF!
WILL ALL OF YOU JUST SHUT UP?!
ALAN'S HARMONIOUS HOME, 7:30 AM.
AND YOU BETTER MAKE THE BUS ON TIME, 'CAUSE I'M NOT GOING TO DRIVE YOU!
YOU CALL THAT DRIVING?! ME STEERING THE WHEEL WHILE YOU SHAVE YOUR SASQUATCH LEGS AND CURL YOUR EYELASHES??
I'D RATHER TAKE THE BUS!
ALAN, APOLOGIZE TO YOUR SISTER FOR CALLING HER A BIGFOOT!!!
SHE HAS TO STOP LOOKING LIKE A HAIRY BEAST FIRST!
I'M OUTTA HERE!

DON'T SLAM THE DOOR!
SLAM!
GOD-- THESE PEOPLE!

AAH...
ANYWAY, IT'S A BEAUTIFUL DAY! JUST PERFECT FOR SWOONING!

I CAN'T BELIEVE YOU!!! YOU HAVE THE NERVE TO MAKE FUN OF ME LIKE THIS?!
HOW CUTE. SHE THINKS I'M SO GREAT THAT I'D ONLY BE JOKING IF I BOTHERED TO ASK HER OUT!

TRY THE USUAL. FLOWERS, PRESENTS... TELL HER HOW YOU FEEL!
THAT'S RIGHT! GOTTA GET BLEU SOME FLOWERS AND TELL HER SHE'S GOING OUT WITH ME THIS FRIDAY!
SNAP
BLEU FINNEGAN, PREPARE TO BE SWEPT OFF YOUR FEET!

BLEU, COME ON. COME OUT OF THERE.
KNOCK KNOCK
NO.
WHY NOT? THINGS CAN'T POSSIBLY GET ANY WORSE THIS WEEK.
WHO CAN TELL HOW MANY PEOPLE HAVE SEEN IT?! ALL OF NORTHERN CALIFORNIA MUST KNOW BY NOW!
FORGET IT, BLEU. THERE'S NOTHING MUCH YOU CAN DO ABOUT IT, IS THERE?
WELL, I'M NOT LEAVING. I'LL JUST LIVE HERE, NEXT TO THE TOILET. TELL MY DAD TO BRING ME MY STUFF AND SOME EXTENSION CORDS.
I'LL NEED MY STEREO TO COVER UP THE FART SOUNDS.
SHOOM
BLEU, IF YOU DON'T GET YER MOPEY ASS OUT OF THE LOO RIGHT NOW I'M GOING TO DRAG YOU OUT AND GIVE YA THE MOST MONSTER WEDGIE YOU'VE EVER DREAMED OF!
... REALLY, YOUR LIFE AIN'T THAT BAD!
YOU THINK?
YEAH, FORGET ABOUT IT. IT'S NO BIG DEAL.
OH, I KNOW! AND MY BOYFRIEND WAS ALL, "I SAW THE TAPE, AND SHE WAS TOTALLY GOING AT HERSELF WITH THIS HUGE BOTTLE OF JOHNSON'S BABY SHAMPOO," AND I WAS ALL "GROOOOSS!"
OMIGOD, THAT'S SO--
PINK STONEWASHED JEANS. THIS HAPPENED.

OP IVY
BAM!
P IVY
OP
COME ON, WEE GIRL. IT'S GOING TO BE A WONDERFUL DAY, I CAN ALREADY FEEL IT.
OP IVY
*THE GO-GO'S "HEAD OVER HEELS"

THUS BEGAN BLEU'S EXCITING DAY!

TOSS
!

YOU AND ME, THIS FRIDAY. HOW ABOUT IT?

DUMP
TRASH

TRASH

SLAM!

BEHOLD! TRUE BEAUTY.

@#$%*!

@#$%*!
FRENCH

!

GRR...

@#$%*!
SCOOP
SCOOP
SCOOP

@#$%*!
CHANK!

TELL ME HOW YOU *REALLY* FEEL, BLEU!
@#$%*!

THERE YOU ARE!

WHAT'S YOUR PROBLEM? YOU AREN'T EVEN TRYING TO SHOW HER YOU LIKE HER!
I CAN'T COMPETE WITH ALAN.
HE HAS MORE MONEY TO GO DO STUFF WITH... BUY HER THINGS...

MAYBE IF YOU TRIED WORKING ON THE WEEKENDS LIKE HE DOES, IT WOULDN'T BE AN ISSUE!
BESIDES, DO YOU REALLY THINK SHE GIVES A SHIT ABOUT MONEY?

DON'T ALL CHICKS WANT THE GUY WITH THE FAT BANK ACCOUNT OVER THE POOR ONE?
GOD, YOU DON'T KNOW ANYTHING ABOUT GIRLS, DO YOU?
THE WORTHWHILE ONES DON'T GIVE A DAMN. BLEU DOESN'T GIVE A DAMN, AND ALAN ISN'T RICH.

YOU CAN'T GET RICH JUST BY WEED-EATING AND BABYSITTING! YOU NEED TO REGISTER AT CLUES INCORPORATED SOMETIME SOON, YOU KNOW THAT?
I TOLD YOU THE OTHER DAY, YOU HAVE TO AT LEAST TRY TO KEEP ALAN FROM DATING HER IF YOU'RE GOING TO BE TOO CHICKEN TO TELL HER HOW YOU FEEL!
YOU'VE SEEN HIM! YOU CAN'T KEEP HIM AWAY FROM HER, OR ANYTHING ELSE IF HE WANTS IT, FOR THAT MATTER...

YOU'RE GOING TO SCREW IT ALL UP AND END UP DATELESS FOR THE REST OF HIGH SCHOOL IF YOU DON'T GET IN GEAR, VICTOR.

WHAT ARE YOU TWO IN A ROW ABOUT?
NOTHING.
NOTHING.

YEAH, OKAY.
ANYWAY, VICTOR... WHERE HAVE YOU BEEN?
WHAT DO YOU MEAN?

YOU HAVEN'T CALLED ME BACK... YA PISSED OFF EARLY FOR SCHOOL... YOU WEREN'T AT THE STUDENT STORE AT BREAK... IT'S NOT LIKE YOU TO JUST DISAPPEAR.
I THOUGHT YOU WERE SICK OR SOMETHIN'.
YOU ALL RIGHT?

I WAS... BUSY.
"BUSY," HE SAYS.
...

AT LEAST YA AREN'T SICK. WELL, WE'RE RENTING SOME MOVIES TONIGHT, AND ME DA SAID YOU WERE INVITED TO COME OVER AND WATCH 'EM, EVEN THOUGH I PROTESTED 'COS YOU'RE DAFT AN' UGLY.
THAT, AND YOU SMELL UP THE PLACE.

SO, YOU WANNA COME OVER, OR WHAT?
NO, THANKS. I'VE, uh, GOT HOMEWORK.

RRRIGHT. 'COS YOU'RE A FECKIN' "A" STUDENT.
WHAT CLIMBED UP YOUR ARSE TODAY?
MAYBE I HAVE OTHER THINGS TO DO, OKAY? MAYBE I DON'T WANT TO HANG OUT WITH YOU ALL THE TIME!!

NO ONE WAS BREAKING YOUR ARM, GOMEZ.

HEY.

...
WHAT'S UP, CLOVER?

HEY, ERIN.
OH, HI.
WHERE'S EVERYONE ELSE? THEY AT THE CAFETERIA?
I SUPPOSE SO.

H-HI, BLEU! Um...
WHAT THE HELL DO YOU WANT, MR. HALF-OF-THE-REASON-FOR-ALL-MY GRIEF-IN-THE-WORLD?

Uh, WELL, I WAS KINDA WONDERING IF YOU WERE BUSY TONIGHT. MY MOM'S MAKING SPAGHETTI, AND--

DID YOU FORGET SOMETHING? YOU'RE ON MY SHIT LIST! YOU CAN'T POSSIBLY MAKE UP FOR WHAT YOU AND ALAN DID! SO THERE'S NO POINT IN YOU TWO TRYING TO KISS UP!
Heh...

VICTOR, WAIT UP!

SQUEAKA
SQUEAKA
ZOOM!

HA HA HA HA HA

FREAK.
HA HAW HA

#Sigh# WHATEVER. COME ON, CLOVER, LET'S GO FOR A WALK.
I DON'T WANT TO HANG AROUND HERE AND RUN INTO ALAN AGAIN... THE BASTARD WON'T LEAVE ME ALONE!
I THOUGHT THIS MORNING WAS BAD ENOUGH. I MEAN, THE BUS RIDE TO SCHOOL WAS JUST HORRIFIC... EVERYONE STILL STARING AT ME... BUT AFTER THE WHOLE BATHROOM THING, IT GOT WORSE! ALAN'S STILL ALL, "BLEU, GO OUT WITH ME FRIDAY!" AND STUFF. THE JOKE'S GONE WAY TOO FAR! I MEAN, FLOWERS IN MY LOCKER, THAT ADAM ANT 45, AND HE EVEN PLANTED LETTERS IN MY NOTEBOOK! I DON'T EVEN KNOW HOW HE DID THAT! AND HE GAVE ME A MIX TAPE, TOO... I UNWOUND THE THING RIGHT IN FRONT OF HIM.
THEN I SAW THERE WAS A REMIX OF "PICTURES OF YOU" ON IT THAT I HAVEN'T HEARD YET, SO I WOUND IT BACK UP WHEN HE LEFT. ≈SNORT≈
...
BLEU, HAS IT EVER OCCURRED TO YOU THAT HE'S REALLY ASKING YOU OUT?
AHEH.
...
AWWWWW, GAAAD!
JUST THROWIN' IT OUT THERE.
BUT HE'S SO LAME! TOTALLY IMMATURE... AND HE'S ALWAYS MAKING FUN OF ME!
ARE YOU BLIND? HE COMPLIMENTS YOU ALL THE TIME, TOO!
OH, GOD, IF IT'S TRUE, THEN I'M EVEN MORE DEPRESSED.
OH, YOUR LIFE IS SO TOUGH, ISN'T IT?! "WAH! BOYS ARE GIVING ME THINGS AND ASKING ME OUT... I JUST WANNA DIE!"
JESUS, CLOVER-- IT'S JUST ONE BOY, AND IT'S ALAN! YOU KNOW HOW I FEEL ABOUT HIM! WHY ARE YOU ACTING LIKE THAT? WHAT'S WRONG?
IT'S NOT JUST AL--
FORGET IT. I GOTTA GO.
WAIT, CLOVER! DUDE, COME ON!
GYM
#BUZZCOCKS "EVER FALLEN IN LOVE?"

WHAT'S EATING HER?
NO ONE'S HERE? THAT'S A FIRST.
FUCK THIS. I'M TAKING THE REST OF THE DAY OFF!
WHAT A DAY. WHAT A *WEEK!*
I NEVER REALLY THOUGHT ALAN WAS *SERIOUSLY* ASKING ME OUT. THAT'S JUST SO *WEIRD!* BUT I *GUESS* THAT MAKES SENSE. WHY ELSE WOULD HE GO TO THE TROUBLE TO DO ALL THAT STUFF FOR ME? NOBODY DOES ALL THAT AS A JOKE. *DUH!*
I SUPPOSE THAT'S WHY CLOVER GOT MAD, BECAUSE I WAS BEING SO MEAN TO ALAN.
WAIT, I CAN'T GO OUT WITH ALAN, THOUGH! THAT'D BE GOING AGAINST HOW I FEEL FOR MR. BISHOP... EVEN IF HE DOESN'T SEE ME THAT WAY. I HAVE TO STAY TRUE TO THE WAY I FEEL, RIGHT?
WHAT AM I SAYING, ANY-WAY? I'D *NEVER* GO OUT WITH ALAN! HE'S ONE OF THE REASONS I'M *IN* SUCH A MESS! HE SHOULD BE HAPPY I CAN EVEN STAND IN THE SAME AREA AS HIM WITHOUT KICKING HIS HEAD OFF!
IF THERE *WAS* ANY CHANCE OF ME GETTING WITH MR. B IN THE FUTURE, IT'S SURE TO BE GONE NOW THAT HE KNOWS ABOUT THAT STUPID VIDEO!

GOD, THIS IS TOO MUCH! THE VIDEO, ALAN, EVERYONE ELSE ACTING WEIRD-- EVEN CLOVER'S BEING A FREAK!

AAAAAGGH!

I SERIOUSLY NEED A PEPSI AND SOME NACHOS.

I THOUGHT SO.

JUST IGNORE THE GIANT OTTER FOLLOWING YOU, BLEU. IT'LL GO AWAY.
NO, IT WON'T.

NO, NO, NO, NO! THIS IS NOT HAPPENING!

GO AWAY!
I MUST BE A LOON. I'M TOTALLY CRAZY!
OH, STOP, WILL YOU?
THAT MAY BE TRUE.

OH, GOD! WOULD YOU SHUT UP?! I DON'T WANT TO HEAR YOU! YOU DON'T EXIST!
OH, YEAH? IF I'M SUCH A FIGMENT OF YOUR IMAGINATION, DON'T YOU THINK YOU SHOULD TELL YOURSELF TO SHUT UP?
YOU CAN'T BE REAL!
CAN'T I? FEEL.

AW, YOU'RE SOFT.
KEEP PETTING ME LIKE THAT AND I WON'T BE!

AGH! GROOOOSS!
WAIT, THAT WAS A JOKE!

HEY!

ZIP

WHOMP!

GOT'CHA!

DO YOU HAVE TO *STARE* LIKE THAT?
NO. POOKAS JUST DO IT TO FREAK PEOPLE OUT. IT'S FUNNY.
WELL, STOP IT.

IF YOU INSIST.
I SWEAR TO GOD, IF YOUR NAME'S *HARVEY,* I'M GONNA LOSE IT.
MY NAME IS *NOT* HARVEY. IT'S NOTHING *LIKE* HARVEY. I *HATE* THAT NAME.
WHAT IS IT THEN?

HENRY.
AAAGH!

I'M KIDDIN'.
WHAT IS IT, REALLY?

HORATIO.
OH, PLEASE.

HOLCOMB?
OH, MY GOD, YOU HAVE THE BIGGEST *ASS!*
YOU'RE *CRUSHING* ME!

YOU GONNA BEHAVE?
JUST GET THE HELL *UP!*
YOU'RE MAKING ME SMELL LIKE *FISHPASTE* WITH YOUR SWEATY OTTER CHEEKS!

BLEU FINNEGAN.
HUMBERT HUMBERT.

WHAT'S *THAT* SUPPOSED TO MEAN?!
JUST A JOKE!
YOU KNOW, THE WHOLE *"H"* THING?

OH, YEAH. HEH.
PARANOID, AREN'T WE?
SHADDAP.

MWAR! GRR!!
OH, RUN! IT'S A BIG SCARY OTTER!
OH GOD, OH GEEZ.

YOU'RE SO ABUSIVE! I'M SO NICE TO YOU, AND YOU JUST HURL OBSCENITIES AT ME AND HURT MY FEELINGS. I'M SENSITIVE, YOU KNOW.
SNIFF
AW, MAN. I REALLY HURT YOUR FEELINGS? I'M SORRY... I DIDN'T MEAN TO...

GREAT, THEN YOU'LL GET ME A SIX PACK OF PABST BLUE RIBBON AND A BAG OF PORK RINDS.
HEY, I'M NOT OLD ENOUGH TO BUY BEER, EVEN WHERE YOU COME FROM! BESIDES, I CAN'T BUY THAT STUFF, IT'S TOO GROSS.

I DOUBT THAT LIQUOR STORE CARRIES FINE CAKES AND FINE WINES, SO PORK SKINS AND BEER ARE GONNA HAVE TO BE GOOD ENOUGH FOR ME. PLEASE?
NO WAY.

PWEEZ?
NO.

I'LL START RECITING EDGAR IF YOU DON'T.
FORGET IT.

"ONCE UPON A MIDNIGHT DREARY, WHILE I PONDERED, WEAK AND WEARY..."
LIQUOR

WHAT'S THE HOLD UP?
KIRIN

THERE'S NO WAY I'M GOING TO BE ABLE TO BUY THE BEER, YOU KNOW. I DON'T EVEN LOOK OLD ENOUGH TO BUY CIGARETTES! THESE GUYS WOULD PROBABLY CARD ME FOR PIXYSTIX, FOR CRYIN' OUT LOUD!

YOU'RE DEPRESSING ME. JUST TAKE IT. I'LL DISTRACT HIM AND YOU RUN OUT THE DOOR.
DOESN'T SOUND LIKE A VERY BRIGHT PLAN. DON'T YOU HAVE A POUCH OR SOME-THING TO PUT THIS IN?
I AIN'T A KANGAROO, KID.

#MAXINE NIGHTENGALE
"RIGHT BACK WHERE WE STARTED FROM"

LUCKY BURGER
TWO STRAWBERRY MILKSHAKES, PLEASE.
SLURP
SLURP
SLURP
SLURP
SLURP SLURP SLURP SLURP
SSLOORP!
POO!
SHRIEK!
POW!
OOOOWW!
SMASH!
YOU WOULDN'T KNOW IT, BUT THEY'RE SINGING YOUNG MC'S "BUST A MOVE" HERE.

THAT WAS FUN. BUT YOU DIDN'T HAVE TO *EAT* THE POLLYWOGS, DID'JA?
HELL, FOR MY PEOPLE, THOSE ARE APPETIZERS.
I COULDN'T RESIST!
* CLASSICS IV "STORMY"
WOW, SO YOU'RE A REAL POOKA, HUH?
I DIDN'T KNOW IF YOU WERE JUST MY *SPIRIT GUIDE* OR SOMETHING.
WHAT ELSE?
NO, THOUGH I *DO* KNOW THE GUY WHO IS... BUT THAT'S ANOTHER STORY.
SO WHAT'S YOUR PROBLEM?
WHAT DO YOU MEAN?
YOU CAN'T FOOL ME. YOU'RE LIKE AN OPEN BOOK. YOU HAD THAT *"I'M ALL ALONE IN THE UNIVERSE"* FACE THIS AFTERNOON. WHAT'S UP?
WELL...
THAT'S IT! I *KNEW* I'D SEEN YOU *SOMEWHERE* BEFORE!
DON'T *SAY* THAT!
YOU KNOW, DID YOU EVER THINK ABOUT DATING THAT ALAN KID ON THE CONDITION YOU GET THE VIDEO FROM HIM?
I CAN'T. IT'D JUST BE TOO WEIRD. AND I DECIDED I HAVE TO BE TRUE TO MR. B.
I GUESS YOU'RE *STUCK*, THEN.
BUT YOU KNOW, IT MAY DO YOU SOME GOOD TO TRY TO GO OUT WITH PEOPLE CLOSER TO YOUR CIRCLE, AGE-WISE AND OTHERWISE-WISE.
THE *AGE* THING! WHY DOES EVERYONE HAVE TO BRING THAT UP? I DON'T CARE ABOUT THAT!
THAT'S NOBLE AND ALL, BUT SERIOUSLY... THINK ABOUT IT.
I'M NOT CHANGING MY MIND ON THIS.
SUIT YOURSELF.
SIGH I WONDER IF CLOVER'S GONNA STAY MAD AT ME?
I DOUBT IT.
CAN'T STAND HAVING HER MAD AT ME.
IT WON'T LAST.
THE SKY'S REALLY CLEAR TONIGHT, ISN'T IT?
BLEU?
ZZZZZZZZZ

LESSEE...
ID... ID...
SNOORE

CROSS
GOOD, A *MEDICAL* CARD.

TRABUCO ROAD... I THINK THAT'S THAT WAY, NEAR THE OLD MINES.
ZZZZZZZZZZ*

WELL, CAN'T LET YOU SLEEP ALL NIGHT IN A FIELD.

BEEP BEEP BEEP
GURUS
7:31
MM?

WAS I DREAMING AGAIN?

WHAT THE HELL *HAPPENED* LAST NIGHT?
WE FOUND YOU ASLEEP ON THE PORCH LAST NIGHT WHEN WE GOT BACK FROM THE THEATER.
I GUESS YOU FORGOT YOUR KEY. COULDN'T GET A WHOLE SENTENCE OUT OF YOU, SO WE PUT YOU TO BED.

GEEZ, I DON'T EVEN REMEMBER HOW I GOT HOME...
HUH. GOTTA CATCH THE BUS! SEE YOU LATER!
SEE YOU, KIDDO!

WHAT HAPPENED TO BLEU YESTERDAY? I DIDN'T SEE HER IN DRAMA OR ANYTHING.
I DON'T KNOW, I WASN'T HERE.

COME TO THINK OF IT, I DIDN'T SEE ANYBODY YESTERDAY AT LUNCH, EXCEPT TOM AND PATRICK. AND WHERE'S CLOVER? I HAVEN'T SEEN EITHER HER OR BLEU TODAY.
HOW AM I SUPPOSED TO KNOW?
HOW DO YOU THINK? ALL I'M SAYIN' IS THAT I BETTER GET AN ANSWER OUT OF BLEU TODAY ABOUT THE DATE. I HAVE TO PLAN WHAT WE'RE GOING TO DO.

JEFFERSON HIGH'S LIBRARY.
LIBRARY

CELTIC MYTHOLOGY.
RELIGION
NORSE
CELTIC
EGYPTIAN GODS
BIG BOOK OF NUTTY MYTHS
OF ANCIENT GREECE & MYTHS
POOKA... POOKA... HERE WE GO.
{Origin: Ireland. Notorious liars and pranksters, Pooka always appear as a giant animal of their choosing, whose characteristics are closest to their personality. They are the clowns of celtic mythology, who take great joy in spreading chaos and staring. You should ditch class and go hang with the big Otter. His real name is Seamus, just so you know.}
RETURN YOUR BOOKS!
SOMETHING VERY FAMILIAR ABOUT THIS.

BLEU!
EEP!

ABOUT TOMORROW... ARE WE ON, OR WHAT?
SORRY, I'M REALLY IN A HURRY.

I'LL TALK TO YOU LATER OR SOMETHING! MAYBE! BYE!
WAIT! WHERE ARE YOU GOING?!

I DON'T GET IT. I DID EVERYTHING I COULD...
I GUESS... I BLEW IT.

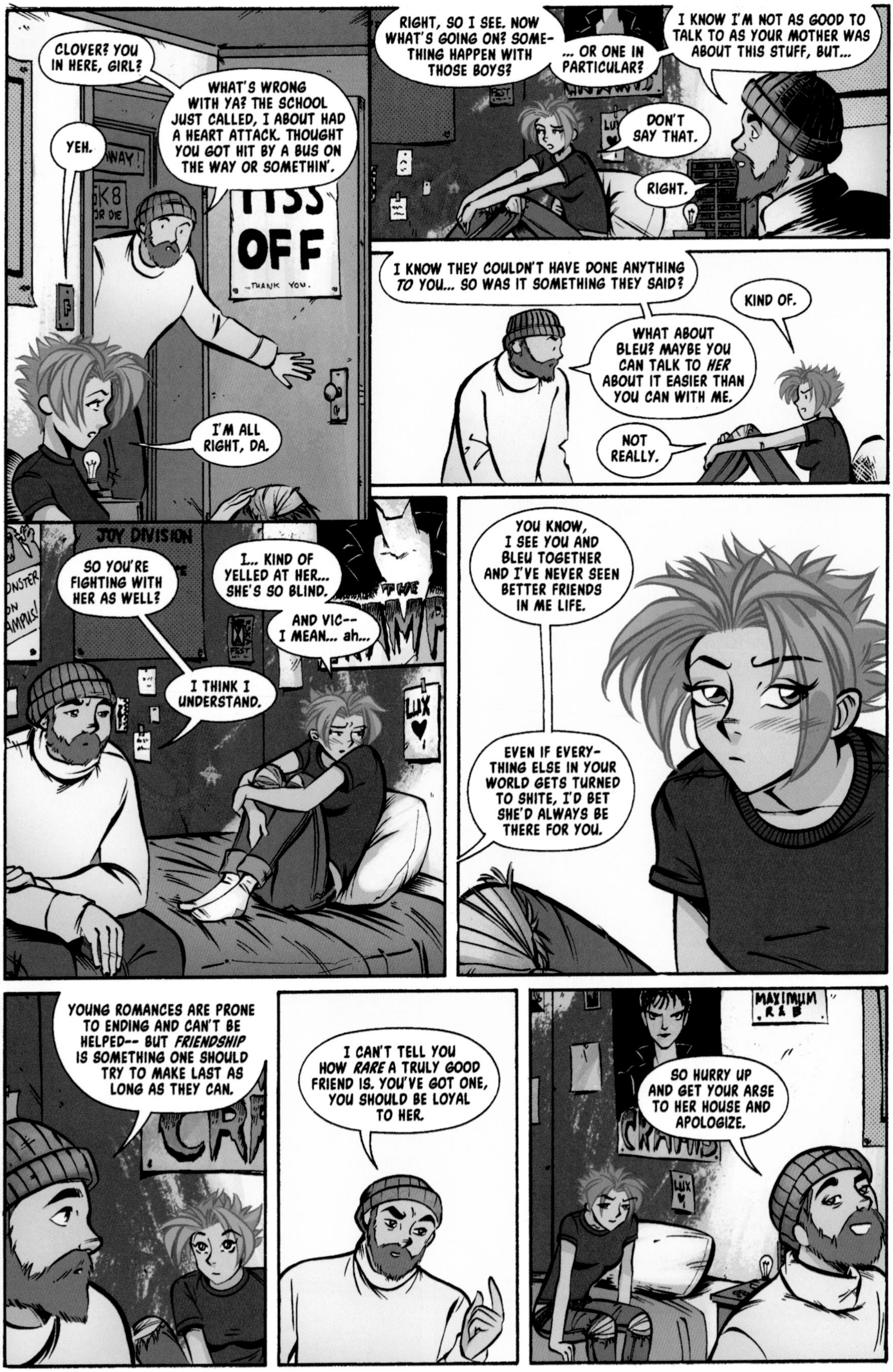

CLOVER? YOU IN HERE, GIRL?

WHAT'S WRONG WITH YA? THE SCHOOL JUST CALLED, I ABOUT HAD A HEART ATTACK. THOUGHT YOU GOT HIT BY A BUS ON THE WAY OR SOMETHIN'.

YEH.

PISS OFF
...THANK YOU.

I'M ALL RIGHT, DA.

RIGHT, SO I SEE. NOW WHAT'S GOING ON? SOMETHING HAPPEN WITH THOSE BOYS?

... OR ONE IN PARTICULAR?

I KNOW I'M NOT AS GOOD TO TALK TO AS YOUR MOTHER WAS ABOUT THIS STUFF, BUT...

DON'T SAY THAT.

RIGHT.

I KNOW THEY COULDN'T HAVE DONE ANYTHING *TO YOU*... SO WAS IT SOMETHING THEY SAID?

KIND OF.

WHAT ABOUT BLEU? MAYBE YOU CAN TALK TO *HER* ABOUT IT EASIER THAN YOU CAN WITH ME.

NOT REALLY.

JOY DIVISION

SO YOU'RE FIGHTING WITH HER AS WELL?

I... KIND OF YELLED AT HER... SHE'S SO BLIND.

AND VIC-- I MEAN... ah...

I THINK I UNDERSTAND.

YOU KNOW, I SEE YOU AND BLEU TOGETHER AND I'VE NEVER SEEN BETTER FRIENDS IN ME LIFE.

EVEN IF EVERYTHING ELSE IN YOUR WORLD GETS TURNED TO SHITE, I'D BET SHE'D ALWAYS BE THERE FOR YOU.

BLEU! I NEVER KNEW! YOU *LUSH!*
WHAT?
OH, HEY! NO WAIT, THIS ISN'T ME...

OH, RIGHT. AND WHAT WAS ALL THAT TALK ABOUT YOU NOT DRINKING AND STUFF?
I SWEAR IT'S NOT ME! IT BELONGS TO *HIM!*

THE POOKA!
WHO?
THE POOKA.
YEAH, HE'S A BIG OTTER!

OH, REALLY! AN IMAGINARY FRIEND, HUH? WHERE IS HE THEN? RIGHT NEXT TO YOU?
NO, HE TOOK OFF FOR A SECOND. I THINK HE HAD TO GO PEE... HE WAS BEHIND THAT TREE.

RIGHT. I LEAVE YOU ALONE FOR A WHOLE AFTERNOON AND YOU COMPLETELY LOSE YOUR MIND.
SEE? THERE HE IS!

...

I DON'T SEE ANYTHING.
REALLY? DAMN, I WAS HOPING AT LEAST *YOU* COULD!
DEFINITELY CANNOT SEE A THING.
YOU'RE NUTS.

WHAT'S SHE TALKING ABOUT? SHE'S *FULL* OF IT! I BET SHE *CAN* SEE ME.
HE SAYS YOU CAN SEE HIM.

WELL, I *CAN'T*. SO TELL YOUR *"FRIEND"* TO SHUT IT.
WHAT ARE YOU DOING UP HERE, ANYWAY?
I WANTED TO SAY I WAS SORRY I FREAKED OUT AT YOU YESTERDAY.

AW, IT'S OKAY...
SLORP
NEVERMIND THAT. IT SHOULDN'T HAVE HAPPENED.
I GUESS I WAS KINDA MEAN TO ALAN...

SO, WHAT ARE YOU GONNA DO ABOUT THE DATE?
I SORT OF BLEW HIM OFF THIS AFTERNOON. I JUST CAN'T DATE HIM!
...
DON'T TELL ME YOU'RE SAVING YOURSELF FOR MR. BISHOP.
SHE IS.

BLEU, DO I NEED TO TELL YOU HOW *RIDICULOUS* THAT IS? NEVERMIND. IT'S ALMOST SIX, AND I'M HUNGRY. WE SHOULD START HEADIN' HOME.

#LULU "TO SIR, WITH LOVE"
SO TELL ME ABOUT THIS MAN YOU'RE AFTER.
MR. BISHOP?
BLEU, DON'T START ON THIS.
OH, HE'S JUST *AMAZING.*

HE'S A TEACHER, BUT HE'S COOL, YOU KNOW? HE DRIVES AN OLD FALCON, IS REALLY SMART... LIKES OLD MOVIES AND GOOD MUSIC...
HE'S *NICE,* TOO. THAT'S A *RARITY* AROUND HERE. AND HE HAS THE SWEETEST SMILE...
I'M GONNA PUKE.

HE'S EVERYTHING I SEE AS *PERFECT.*
"PERFECT"?
I'D *NEVER* HAVE THE TROUBLES I HAVE RIGHT NOW IF HE WAS *OUR* AGE AND I HUNG OUT WITH HIM ALL THE TIME.
HE'D *PROTECT* MY REPUTATION, NOT THINK OF NEW WAYS TO *TARNISH* IT!

WE'D HAVE *PICNICS* TOGETHER...
YEAH, YOU AND YOUR EGG SALAD SANDWICHES WOULD MAKE FOR GREAT *KISSY BREATH.*
...AND STROLL AROUND THE LAKE IN THE MOONLIGHT...
IF IT'S *BASS LAKE* YOU'RE TALKIN' ABOUT, YOU BETTER HAVE *NOSE PLUGS,* TOO. IT'S LIKE A *SEWAGE DUMP.*
...WE'D DANCE AT THE OLD BALLROOM UNTIL DAWN...
DANCE TO *WHAT?* THEY CLOSE AT *11:00.*
IT'D BE *MAGICAL.*
MORE LIKE *TRAGICAL.*

SINCE WE'RE HERE, WE SHOULD GRAB SOME SODAS FOR THE TREK HOME.
WHAT'S WRONG?

...
IS THAT...? YES, IT *IS.*

IT APPEARS THAT YOUR PERFECT MAN IS PERFECTLY *TAKEN.*
SO IT DOES!

FINE! SEE IF I CARE!
BLEU!
GRR...
WHERE ARE YOU GOING???

THIS HAS GOT TO BE *YOUR* FAULT.

A-HA!

AND SO...
ALAAAAN! GET THE DOOR!!!

BLEU!? HEY--
ALAN, I'LL GO OUT WITH YOU ON ONE CONDITION--
YOU GIVE ME THAT STUPID TAPE TOMORROW!

Uh, SURE...
GOOD! SEE YOU THEN!

SHE LOVES ME.
WHAT THE HELL DID I JUST DO?

Chapter Four
"Hands Off... She's Mine"

*Illustration inspired by actual quote from original edition editor, Jamie S. Rich.

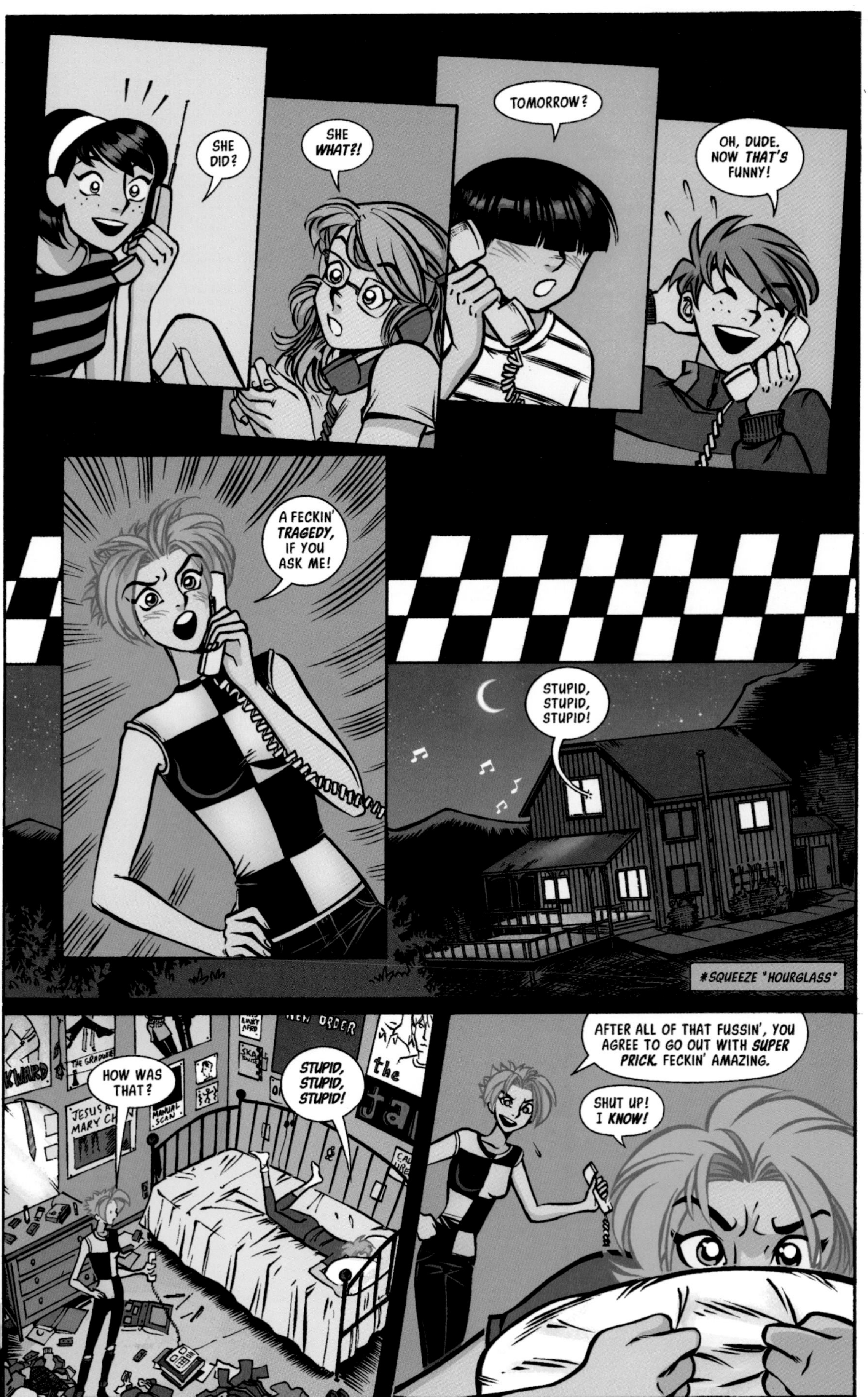
SHE DID?
SHE WHAT?!
TOMORROW?
OH, DUDE. NOW THAT'S FUNNY!
A FECKIN' TRAGEDY, IF YOU ASK ME!
STUPID, STUPID, STUPID!
*SQUEEZE "HOURGLASS"
HOW WAS THAT?
STUPID, STUPID, STUPID!
AFTER ALL OF THAT FUSSIN', YOU AGREE TO GO OUT WITH SUPER PRICK FECKIN' AMAZING.
SHUT UP! I KNOW!

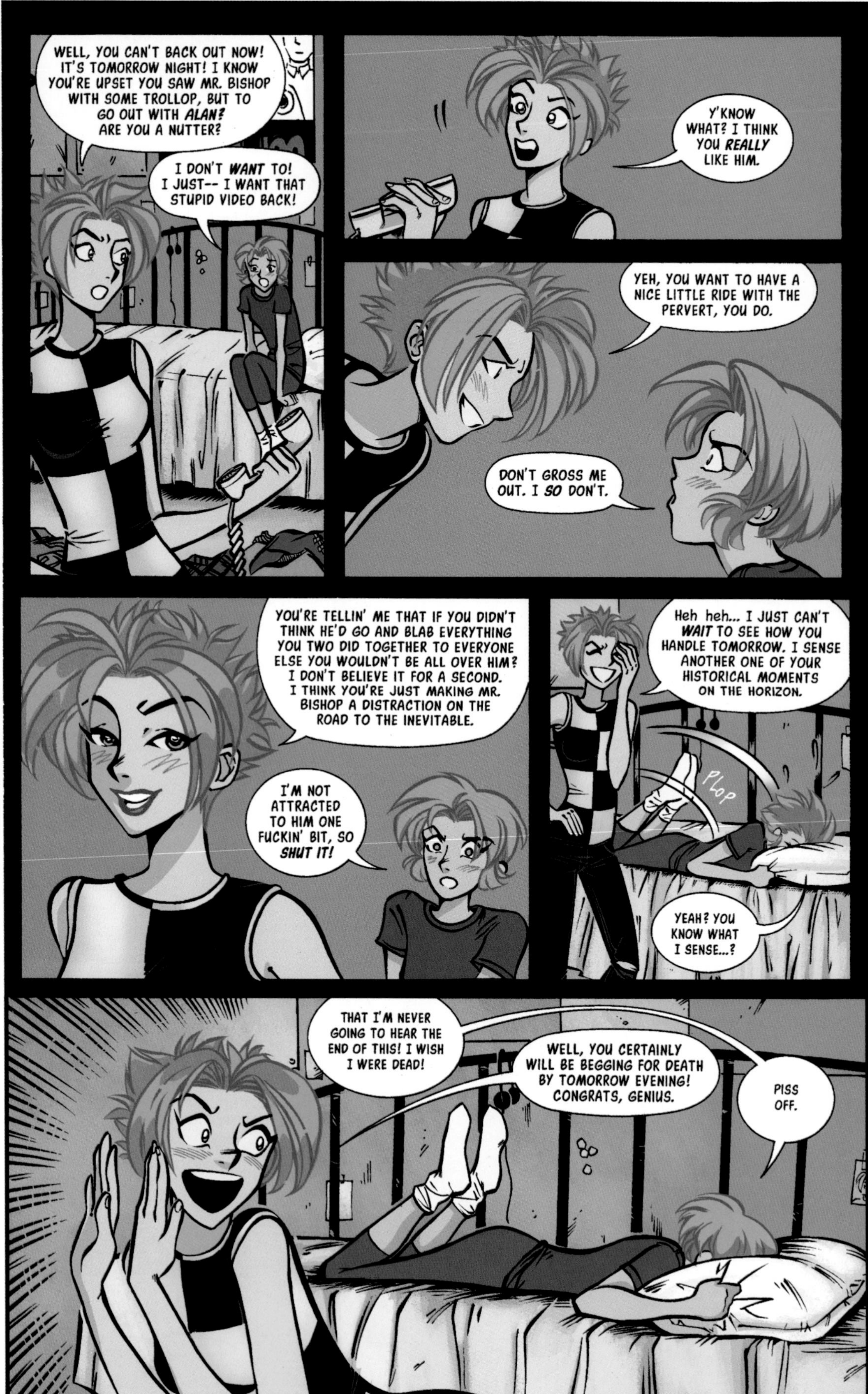

WELL, YOU CAN'T BACK OUT NOW! IT'S TOMORROW NIGHT! I KNOW YOU'RE UPSET YOU SAW MR. BISHOP WITH SOME TROLLOP, BUT TO GO OUT WITH ALAN? ARE YOU A NUTTER?
I DON'T WANT TO! I JUST-- I WANT THAT STUPID VIDEO BACK!
Y'KNOW WHAT? I THINK YOU REALLY LIKE HIM.
YEH, YOU WANT TO HAVE A NICE LITTLE RIDE WITH THE PERVERT, YOU DO.
DON'T GROSS ME OUT. I SO DON'T.
YOU'RE TELLIN' ME THAT IF YOU DIDN'T THINK HE'D GO AND BLAB EVERYTHING YOU TWO DID TOGETHER TO EVERYONE ELSE YOU WOULDN'T BE ALL OVER HIM? I DON'T BELIEVE IT FOR A SECOND. I THINK YOU'RE JUST MAKING MR. BISHOP A DISTRACTION ON THE ROAD TO THE INEVITABLE.
I'M NOT ATTRACTED TO HIM ONE FUCKIN' BIT, SO SHUT IT!
Heh heh... I JUST CAN'T WAIT TO SEE HOW YOU HANDLE TOMORROW. I SENSE ANOTHER ONE OF YOUR HISTORICAL MOMENTS ON THE HORIZON.
PLOP
YEAH? YOU KNOW WHAT I SENSE...?
THAT I'M NEVER GOING TO HEAR THE END OF THIS! I WISH I WERE DEAD!
WELL, YOU CERTAINLY WILL BE BEGGING FOR DEATH BY TOMORROW EVENING! CONGRATS, GENIUS.
PISS OFF.

TAP
TAP
ERIN! MONKEY JUST CALLED ME--
I KNOW, I KNOW. CALM DOWN. BLEU AGREED TO THE DATE THING ON THE CONDITION SHE GOT THE TAPE BACK... CLOVER TOLD ME ALL ABOUT IT.
BUT, I MEAN, YOU WERE *RIGHT!* I NEVER THOUGHT SHE'D GO FOR IT!
I CAN'T BELIEVE IT!
EASY, FREAKCHILD. WHO HAS THE VIDEO, YOU OR ALAN?
ALAN.
HMM, SO WE CAN'T KEEP THAT FROM HIM TO PREVENT THE DATE... THAT WOULD BE TOO SIMPLE, WOULDN'T IT?
OKAY. IT'S GOING TO BE A BIT HARDER, BUT I THINK WE CAN MANAGE...
WE'RE ALL PRETTY CREATIVE. WELL, *I* AM ANYWAY.
GET MONKEYBOY OVER HERE AFTER SCHOOL TOMORROW, AND WE'LL GO FROM THERE.
IN THE MEANTIME...
"... FIND OUT WHAT HIS PLAN IS, AND BE *COOL* ABOUT IT. GOT IT?"
"YEAH."
KNOK
KNOK
K-NOK

HEY, VICTOR. COME ON IN. WHAT'S UP?
NOTHIN', JUST BORED. WHAT ARE YOU DOING?
I'M DECIDING WHAT BLEU AND I ARE GONNA DO TOMORROW NIGHT.
OH, YEAH, I HEARD SHE FINALLY SAID SHE'D GO OUT WITH YOU. ***CONGRATULATIONS.***
SO, WHAT, YOU DIDN'T ASK HER WHAT SHE WANTED TO DO?
I KNOW WHAT SHE'D SAY. I'D GO, "WHAT DO YOU WANT TO DO?" AND SHE'D GO, "I DON'T KNOW, WHAT DO YOU WANT TO DO?" AND THEN NOTHING WOULD HAPPEN.
WHAT ARE YOU DOING, THEN?
I WAS CHECKING OUT THE OL' TOWER THEATER, IT LOOKS LIKE THEY'RE HAVING A MARILYN MONROE FESTIVAL. I KNOW BLEU LIKES HER, SO WE'LL HIT THE DOUBLE FEATURE AFTER DINNER. OTHERWISE, THERE'S NOT REALLY MUCH OF A CHOICE.
Huh, THE TOWER, Eh? THAT'S COOL. YOU GOING FOR ITALIAN?
FOOT FETISH
OF COURSE. I HAVE RESERVATIONS ALREADY AT GAMBINO'S.
HOW ARE YOU GONNA GET THERE? YOUR MOM ACTUALLY GOING TO LET YOU BORROW THE CAR?
FOOT FETISH
HELL, NO. I HAVE ANOTHER PLAN... BUT I AIN'T SAYIN' WHAT IT IS, IN CASE IT DOESN'T WORK OUT.
DON'T TELL ME YOU...
Shh! NOT ANOTHER WORD!

DON'T YOU THINK IT'S KIND OF SHITTY THAT SHE'D ONLY GO OUT WITH YOU IF YOU GAVE HER THE VIDEO?

NOT AT ALL. I KNEW SHE'D TAKE SOME SORT OF ANGLE LIKE THAT, JUST TO COVER UP HOW MUCH SHE WANTS TO GO WITH ME. I DON'T CARE.

YEAH... YOU'RE PROBABLY RIGHT. I'M SURE SHE'S COUNTING THE MINUTES TILL SHE CAN SEE YOU AGAIN.

AND SO FRIDAY CAME, AND OUR HEROINE AVOIDED ALAN WITH MUCH SUCCESS.
*INXS "THE ONE THING"

THAT IS, UNTIL...

SHIT!

WHAT THE HELL IS HE DOING ON MY BUS?!

FUMP!

SHWP
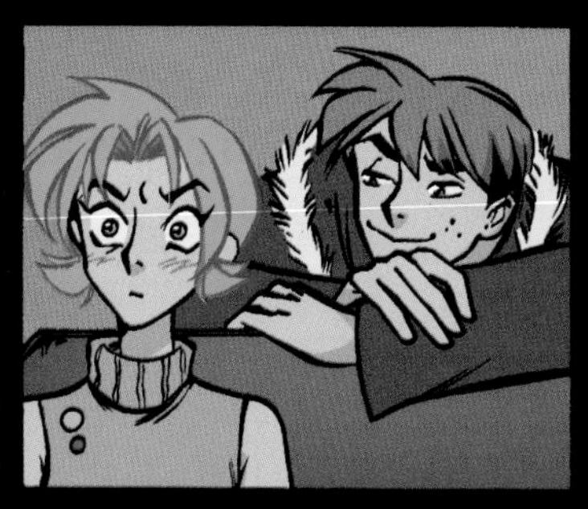

OH, LOOK! IT'S MY STOP!

SEE YOU AT SIX.
>GRUNT<

HOY.
OOOH...
STOP SULKING AND GET READY FOR YOUR STUPID DATE, BLEU.
CLOVERRRR, WHAT IF HE GOES AND TRIES TO PLANT HIS FLAPPY CAKE-POCKET ON ME?
KISS HIM BACK, 'COS YOU KNOW YOU WANT TO.
FUCK OFF!
GO PICK OUT YOUR COSTUME, YOU FOKIN' CLOWN.
WHAT THE HELL AM I GOING TO WEAR?
DOES IT REALLY MATTER HOW YOU LOOK?
NO! YES-- ARG!
WHY DON'T YOU JUST DRESS UP LIKE YOU WERE GOING TO A CONCERT? THAT'S EASY ENOUGH.
YEAH...
Hmm... GUESS THIS CAN GO WITH THIS...
WHAT'S THAT ODOR? THAT'S OBSCENE!
YOU SURE IT WASN'T SOME ANXIETY FUMES COMING FROM YOU?
HELL, NO! THAT WASN'T ME! WHAT IS THAT COMING FROM?!
JEZUS-GAD! THAT'S HORRIBLE! MY GOD!!
CHRIST! SMELLS LIKE YOUR CLOSET HAS BEEN SMUGGLING HAMS!
DEXY'S MIDNIGHT RUNNERS

WHEEEEEEEWW!
AAA!
FUCKING HELL, I LOOK *SMASHING* IN THIS GET-UP!!!
DON'T *DO* THAT!
YOU KNOW YOU MISSED ME. WHADDAYA THINK?
I THINK YOU'RE GONNA SIT THE HELL DOWN AND KEEP YOUR ASS TO YOURSELF!
BUT I HAD TO GET READY FOR THE DATE!
YOU *WHAT?*
YOU NEED A CHAPERONE YOUNG LADY!
I AM COMING WITH YOU!
ASS AND ALL.
THE HELL YOU ARE! YOU'RE STAYING HERE WITH CLOVER!
Shove
OH, WE COULDN'T ALLOW THAT.
YOU NEED PROTECTION!
YEAH, YOU WANT THAT "FLAPPY CAKE-POCKET" KEPT AWAY FROM YOU, DON'T YA?

OKAY, FINE.
I CAN TELL WHEN I'M NOT WANTED.
Ah, NOW LOOK WHAT YOU'VE DONE, FINNEGAN. YOU SHOULDN'T MESS WITH A POOKA LIKE THAT. YOU DON'T KNOW WHAT HAPPENS WHEN YOU HURT THEIR FEELINGS.
OH, ALL RIGHT.
I KNEW YOU THOUGHT I WAS SEXY!
WUMP!
YOU AREN'T INVITED!
OKAY, OKAY. I UNDERSTAND! I'M NOT INVITED ON YOUR DATE.
THAT HURT, FINNEGAN?
BUT I CAN CRASH IT, RIGHT?
BY ALL MEANS.
DEXY'S MIDNIGHT RUNNERS
HALF AN HOUR LATER...
I THOUGHT SHE HATED THIS ALAN KID?
YOU NEVER CAN REALLY TELL...
DEXY'S MIDNIGHT RUNNERS
WHAT DO YOU GUYS THINK?
I WOULDN'T HAVE ADVISED A SKIRT, BUT YOU LOOK GOOD.
HOPE YOU HAVE YOUR CHASTITY BELT ON, KID.

MAN! THIS STUPID HELMET MAKES ME LOOK LIKE A MUSHROOM!

OR A PEEN... KINDA LIKE JAMIE... Jamie J. Peen-Sammich.

VROOOM
SCRTCH
BUMP!
OOF.
VROOOM
SCRTCH
WOULD YOU STOP THAT?!
WHAT? THERE SEEMS TO BE A PROBLEM WITH THE BRAKE. IT KEEPS STICKING.
SCRTCH
GRR
BUMP
OOH, YEAH!
QUIT IT! YOU'RE DIRTY!
JUST MESSING AROUND, DON'T GET ALL BENT.
BEAUTIFUL!
THIS IS WAY BETTER THAN I'D IMAGINED! TOO BAD IT'S NOT WITH MR. B., BUT THIS'LL DO...
WHERE ARE WE GOING, ANYWAY?
YOU'LL SEE.

GAMBINO'S
VICTOR, THEY HERE YET?
NO, NOT-- WAIT.
THAT BASTARD! HE DID GET ONE!
OOH, HE'S PRETTY SLICK, ISN'T HE?
WELL, WE'RE JUST GOING TO HAVE TO MAKE UP FOR HIS CLEVERNESS WITH A BIT OF SABOTAGE. COME ON.
ISN'T THIS PLACE EXPENSIVE?
IT'S NOT AS BAD AS SOME, AND THE FOOD IS SUPPOSED TO KICK ASS. DON'T WORRY ABOUT IT.
POOR LITTLE GUYS. DID YOU KNOW THEY MAKE A SCREAMING SOUND WHEN YOU PUT THEM IN BOILING WATER? IT'S HORRIBLE.
THEY'RE SOAKED IN WINE BEFORE THEY COOK THEM...
... THEY'RE DRUNK AND PROBABLY JUST SQUEALING AFTER HEARING SOME DUMB JOKE ONE OF THE OTHER LOBSTERS TOLD THEM BEFORE THEY WERE TAKEN AWAY. THEY DON'T FEEL A THING.
IF WE LIVED BY THE OCEAN, I'D LIBERATE THEM.
YEAH, YOU'D LIBERATE THEM FROM THEIR SHELLS, DIP THEM IN GARLIC BUTTER, AND EAT THE LITTLE BASTARDS RIGHT QUICK IS WHAT YOU'D DO.
CAN I JUST SAY THAT BLACK REBEL MOTORCYCLE CLUB'S "RIFLES" FUCKIN' ROCKS > MY GOD! I LOVE THIS BAND!

THIS PLACE IS TOO FANCY. I FEEL LIKE I'M STICKING OUT LIKE A SORE THUMB.
HAVE YOU NOTICED YOUR HAIR IN THE LAST FIFTEEN YEARS? YOU STICK OUT LIKE A SORE THUMB EVERYWHERE YOU GO, KID. GET USED TO IT.

RESERVATION FOR WALSH.
Mmm. YES... THIS WAY.

WHAT'S THIS? NO, NO, NO, I'D LIKE A WINDOW SEAT.
I'M SORRY, WE DON'T HAVE ANY WINDOW SEATS AVAILABLE AT THE MOMENT.

WHAT DO YOU CALL THOSE, THEN? HMM?
RESERVED.

YEAH? WELL, I AM NOT SITTING NEXT TO THE KITCHEN. I WANT A DECENT TABLE!
Um, ALAN, THIS TABLE IS FINE...

NO, IT'S NOT. WE'RE NOT SITTING HERE. WE WON'T BE HIDDEN IN A CORNER, I WANT TO BE IN FULL VIEW OF ANYONE THAT COMES IN HERE.
THEY THINK WE'RE PUNK TRASH OR SOMETHING, AND I WON'T PUT UP WITH IT.

ALAN, SERIOUSLY, I ALREADY FEEL WEIRD HERE...
FOLLOW ME THIS WAY, PLEASE.
SSHT!

THERE, ARE YOU HAPPY? NOW EVERYONE CAN WATCH THE CIRCUS FREAKS EAT FETTUCCINE.
FLAP

YOUR MENUS. WOULD YOU LIKE TO HEAR OUR SPECIALS OF THE EVENING?
NO, WE CAN AFFORD THE REGULAR MENU ITEMS, THANKS.
ALAN, HE'S SUPPOSED TO ASK US THAT.

I KNOW, BUT I FIND IT INSULTING. IT'S NOT LIKE WE SHOWED UP WITH COUPONS OR ANYTHING.
WHAT'S WRONG WITH COUPONS?

WHAT'S WRONG WITH COUP--?
EXCUSE ME, WAITER? THE LADY WOULD LIKE TO KNOW TONIGHT'S WELFARE SPECIALS. SHE'S REALLY CONCERNED ABOUT SAVING MY MONEY, GOD BLESS HER.
FINE, FORGET THE SPECIALS...

JUST KEEP OUT OF THE WAY OF THE SERVERS AND TRY NOT TO SET THE RESTAURANT ON FIRE, OKAY?
OKAY, PAULIE.

HOW DO YOU KNOW THIS GUY AGAIN?
I TAKE HIS SATURDAY COOKING CLASS AT THE COLLEGE WORKSHOP. I'M HIS BEST STUDENT!
PLUS HE OWES ME FROM POKER NIGHT.
FANTASTIC.

ARE YOU READY TO ORDER?
YES. GO AHEAD, BLEU.
Um, I'LL JUST HAVE THE CHICKEN ALFREDO.

THAT'S IT? YOU DON'T WANT LOBSTER OR FILET MIGNON WITH YOUR ALFREDO?
CHICKEN IS FINE. CHICKEN IS GROOVY. *I-AM-HAVING-THE-CHICKEN.*

ALL RIGHT, THEN. I'LL HAVE THE-- NO, WAIT, WHAT'S IN THE-- NO, I DON'T THINK I WANT THAT.
DO YOU NEED MORE TIME, SIR?
NO, I DON'T. I'M READY. I'LL HAVE THE-- THE-- Uh, HOW DO YOU SAY...
GAMBINO'S
ARE YOU SURE?
NOTHING "SUCKS" HERE, SIR.
WHY, DOES IT SUCK?
I'LL HAVE THE OTHER ONE, THEN.
GAMBINO'S

YES?
THIS ONE.
VERY GOOD.
NO, THIS ONE.
GAMBINO'S

OF COURSE.
WITH NO SHRIMP. I CAN'T EAT SHRIMP, I'M REALLY ALLERGIC TO THEM, SO PLEASE MAKE SURE THERE'S NONE IN IT.
GAMBINO'S
DID HE SAY *EXTRA* SHRIMP? COMING RIGHT UP, ALAN DEAR.

SNEAKY SHRIMP
CHOMP
GULP
MOTHERFUCKER!
THERE'S NO WAY AROUND IT! I'M GONNA BREAK OUT IN HIVES! BASTARDS!

WHAT'S WRONG?
DO YOU WANT TO MOVE? YOU LOOK UNCOMFORTABLE.

I'M FINE, I DON'T WANT TO MOVE AGAIN!
CRINGE
I DON'T WANT YOU UNCOMFORTABLE, BECAUSE THEN YOU WON'T EAT YOUR CHEAP SPECIAL AND ALL THAT OVERCOOKED PASTA WILL GO TO WASTE. WAITER!

PLAYING DEAF, IS HE? MIGHT AS WELL, HE ALREADY HAS DUMB COVERED.
BAM
DICKHEAD, HE CAN HEAR YOU!

MAY I ASSIST YOU WITH SOMETHING, SIR?
THE LADY IS UNCOMFORTABLE, SHE WOULD LIKE TO BE SEATED AT ANOTHER TABLE.

I DON'T BLAME HER.
I MEAN WITH ME!

I'M FINE... REALLY.
NO, YOU'RE NOT. WE NEED TO MOVE.

YOU KNOW, IT SEEMS TO ME THAT ALAN IS DOING ENOUGH TO SCREW UP THEIR DATE BY HIMSELF. HE DOESN'T REALLY NEED OUR HELP...
BUT IT'S KINDA FUN TO WATCH IT GO AWRY, ISN'T IT?
Mmm, YEAH, IT IS.

WHAT THE HELL IS ALAN DOING NOW? PROBABLY GETTING HIS ASS BEAT UP IN THE BACK OF THE RESTAURANT.

Ping
THIS SEAT TAKEN?
AAA! YES! PISS OFF!

TUT-TUT. I'M SURE I'M A FAR BETTER DATE THAN THIS ALAN KID.
THAT'S NOT THE POINT! I SAID-- OKAY, ALAN'S ON HIS WAY BACK, NOW GET LOST!

I SEE HOW YOU ARE.
SOME OTHER BOY JUST WALTZES UP OUT OF NOWHERE AND YOUR ADORING POOKA IS OUT OF THE PICTURE. YOU'RE SO FICKLE.

Y'BITCH.
SMAK!

ZOOM
I TOLD YOU TO GET LOST, DAMMIT!
I AM LOST. I CAN'T FIND MY WAY OUT FROM UNDER THE TABLE.

HAVING SOME SPASMS OVER HERE, BLEU?
I'M JUST PEACHY, NO PROBLEM HERE.

← POOKA TOESES

DON'T SCRATCH YOURSELF, ALAN... DON'T SCRATCH!
YOU SCRATCH, THE BUMPS GET HUGE, YOU GROSS OUT THE GIRL, YOU GET NOTHING FOR ALL YOUR EFFORTS TONIGHT.

RUB
RUB
RUB

ON SECOND THOUGHT... YOW, YOU'RE A MORE ADVENTUROUS THAN I THOUGHT
HUH?

BLEU, I APPRECIATE WHAT YOU'RE DOING, REALLY... BUT HAVE YOU EVER CONSIDERED SHAVING THEM HOBBIT FEET OF YOURS?
I DON'T KNOW WHAT YOU'RE TALKING ABOUT!
YES, YOU DO.

Uh, MAYBE THERE'S A BIG... RAT... OR A YETI, UNDER THE TABLE. OR SOMETHING.
JUST A SECOND, I'LL CHECK FOR YOU.
SCRATCH
SCRATCH

ROAR!
Rollerskates →

PURE EVIL ↓ HEY, CHYNNA! GOT ENOUGH PANELS JAMMED INTO THE LAST HALF OF THIS STUPID BOOK?!

IS HE ILL? HE JUST MISSED HIS CUE TO SAY SOMETHING VULGAR.
SHH!

HEY, YOU ASKED ME THE QUESTION! JESUS!
HA-HA! OKAY, OKAY, I'LL KEEP QUIET.

SHE DOESN'T SEEM TO NOTICE THE HIVES... MAYBE I CAN STILL GET SOME-WHERE TONIGHT!

POP

BWAAAARP!
WOAH-HO-HO! PARDON MY FRENCH!

OH, JAYSUS! I THINK I STAINED ME KILT!
THAT'S MY DAD'S KILT! YOU BETTER NOT RUIN IT!

UH-UH. THAT SO WAS NOT ME...

OH, GOD! WHAT THE HELL DID YOU EAT?!
ME?! I COULDN'T PRODUCE A STENCH LIKE THAT IF I TRIED!
JUST A BIT OF HEAD CHEESE AND BUTTERMILK... GAW...

OH, GOD... I MAY PUKE...
HEY, WHERE'S EVERYONE GOING?

Y'KNOW, BLEU, THIS WOULD BE A GREAT TECHNIQUE ON A CROWDED DANCE FLOOR.
I CAN'T WAIT FOR YOUR PROM.
I'M JUST GONNA PRETEND THAT DIDN'T HAPPEN.
I SWEAR TO YOU, THAT WASN'T MY ASS.

!
IT'S OKAY, I UNDERSTAND.
GIRLS FART, TOO.

I JUST HOPE CUTTING THOSE GODZILLA-SIZED AIR BISCUITS AREN'T A HOBBY OF YOURS.

ITCH, ITCH, ITCH!

I'LL BE RIGHT BACK...
YEAH, OKAY.

WHERE IS ALAN OFF TO?
PERHAPS HIS ALLERGIES ARE GETTING TO HIM?
OH, LORELEI
MAYBE IT'S TIME TO PUT HIM INTO QUARANTINE.
YEAH.

SCRATCH
SCRATCH
SCRATCH
GAH!

OH, NO! I LOOK LIKE THE FUCKING *ELEPHANT MAN!*

THE FRENCH ARE GLAD TO... DIE FOR LOVE... THEY DELIGHT IN FIGHT-ING DUELS...
BUT I PREFER A MAN WHO LIIIVES AND GIIIIVES-EXPENSIVE-JEWELS!

AW, HELL, SOMEONE'S COMING...
CREEEAK

VWIP

A KISS ON THE HAND MAY BE QUITE CONTINENTAL, BUT DIAMONDS ARE A GIRL'S BEST FRIEND...

THAT SHOULD DO IT.

A KISS MAY BE GRAND, BUT IT WON'T PAY THE RENTAL ON YOUR HUMBLE FLAT, OR HELP YOU AT THE AUTO-MAT!
FUCK! LOCK WON'T OPEN!

MEN GROW COLD AS GIRLS GROW OLD, AND WE ALL LOSE OUR CHARMS IN THE END...
...BUT SQUARE-CUT OR PEAR-SHAPED, THESE ROCKS DON'T LOSE THEIR SHAPE! DIAMONDS ARE A GIRL'S BEST FRIEND!

THAT LOOKS EASY ENOUGH.
TIFFANY'S!

CARTIER!

SONOFABITCH!
LEAP!
SNAG

HE'S YOUR GUY WHEN STOCKS ARE HIIIGH, BUT BEWARE WHEN THEY START TO DESCEND--
-- IT'S THEN THAT THOSE LOUSES GO BACK TO THEIR SPOUSES... DIAMONDS ARE A GIRL'S BEST FRIEND!
SSH!
SHUT UP!

...TIME ROLLS ON, AND YOUTH IS GONE... AND YOU CAN'T STRAIGHTEN UP WHEN YOU BEND-- BUT STIFF BACK OR STIFF KNEES--
GRR...

YOU STAND STRAIGHT AT TIIIFFFANY'S!
RIP
BAM

FUCK... MY ANKLE!
WAAAGH! SCARY MONSTER MAN'S GONNA EAT ME!
COME ALONG, DEAR!
DIAMOOOOONDS...
DIAAMOOOONDS...
BEST FRIEEEEND!
MAN, YOU MISSED THE BEST PART!
FROMP

LIMP
LIMP
LIMP
THE KINKS
I DON'T MEAN RHINESTONES, BUT DIAMOOONDS-- ARE A GIRL'S BEST-

AND YOUR SEAT!
IF THAT WAS THE BEST PART, I'M GOING HOME RIGHT FUCKING NOW.

GOD, VICTOR. DID YOU TRY TO KILL HIM?
YOU KIDDING? I JUST SHUT THE DOOR, THAT'S IT.

AND SO...
I CAN'T BELIEVE YOU STAINED MY DAD'S KILT... HE'S GONNA THROTTLE ME!
I'M SORRY! HERE, JUST LET ME PUT SOME SOAP ON THE STAIN FOR YA!
BUTTER

NOOO! STUPID! DON'T PUT BUTTER ON WOOL, YOU MORON!
SQUORKA SQUORKA
SPLOOSH
BUTTER

MORON?! STUPID?!? MOI??? YOU KNOW WHAT? THAT'S IT! ENOUGH ABUSE OUT OF YOU.
I'M GOING BACK HOME! I'M OUT OF HERE, YOUNG LADY!
WHAT, GOING BACK TO IRELAND ALREADY?

YES! RIGHT NOW! GOOD-BYE!
WAIT, SEAMUS...!
NO MORE!

COME ON BLEU, LET'S GO!

WHAT'S THE RUSH? I THOUGHT YOU WANTED TO TAKE YOUR TIME HANGING OUT.
TUG
I DON'T FEEL SO HOT, BLEU. I THINK WE'RE GOING TO HAVE TO CUT THIS SHORT AFTER ALL.

BLEU! I FIGURED THE MARILYN FESTIVAL WOULD BE YOUR KIND OF THING. HOW ARE YOU?
I-I'M JUST GREAT!

...
OH, THIS IS MY SISTER, JANET. JANET, THIS IS BLEU, ONE OF MY STUDENTS AT JEFFERSON.
NICE TO MEET YOU, BLEU.
THE KINKS

YOUR SISTER?
SHOVE

THE PLEASURE'S ALL MINE!

OH, SORRY. THIS IS ALAN WALSH. I THINK YOU'VE MET HIM BEFORE, MR. B.

ARE YOU ALL RIGHT, ALAN? IT LOOKS LIKE YOU HAD A PRETTY SEVERE REACTION TO SOMETHING...
YEAH, SMALL POX.

JESUS, WHEN DID ALL THIS HAPPEN TO YOU?
I'VE BEEN LOOKING LIKE THIS MOST OF THE NIGHT, BLEU.
BARRING THE SPRAINED ANKLE I GOT WHEN I FELL OUT THE WINDOW.

HA-HA-HA! ALAN, SUCH A KIDDER. WELL, WE'LL BE SEEING YOU AROUND, MR. B.! LATER!
UH, BYE...

BUURR--
KLIK
BUURR--
KLIK
FUCK!
SIGH...

YOU SURE WE SHOULDN'T GET YOU TO A HOSPITAL OR SOMETHING?
I'M FINE. LOOKS LIKE WE'RE WALKING HOME TONIGHT.

I'D CALL MY DAD TO COME AND PICK US UP, BUT HE WON'T BE BACK UNTIL LATE. WHAT ABOUT YOUR PARENTS?
YEAH, RIGHT. I WOULDN'T COUNT ON IT. LET'S GET MOVING.

AN UNGODLY AMOUNT OF TIME LATER.
LIMP
LIMP
LIMP

WELL... HERE WE ARE.
IT'S BEEN A MEMORABLE NIGHT, TO SAY THE LEAST. SORRY YOU GOT ALL FUCKED UP, ALAN.

Um, HOW ABOUT THAT TAPE?

THANKS.

WELL... GOODNIGHT, THEN.
THE KINKS
BODDINGTONS
SAFE AT LAST! I'M GOING TO HAVE FUN BURNING YOUR ASS! HEY, CLOVER, C'MERE!
VICTOR'S PLACE.
OH, UH, HEY DUDE... HOW DID THE DATE GO?
HOW DOES IT FUCKING LOOK LIKE IT WENT?
IT WAS BEYOND A DISASTER. THAT GIRL IS A LOON! Y'GOT ANY NEOSPORIN?
DID YOU GIVE BLEU THE TAPE?
I GAVE HER A TAPE, BUT NOT THE TAPE. I AIN'T STUPID, I KNEW SHE'D TRASH IT.
MADE ANOTHER COPY FOR YOUR RECORDS AS WELL. HERE YOU GO.
YES!!!
YOU KNOW, WITH ALL THE EQUIPMENT YOU'VE SWIPED FROM ADVANCED RADIO/TELEVISION CLASS AND HOW CLEVER YOU ARE WITH THIS SORT OF THING, I WONDER WHY WE COULDN'T PIRATE THIS ONTO CHANNEL 13?
I MEAN, I THINK ALL OF FRESBURGER AND DEADWOOD WOULD LOVE TO SEE SOME GOOD NUDITY ON THEIR FAVORITE LOCAL T.V. STATION.
SOMEWHERE AROUND 3 A.M.
...AND THEN SEAMUS JUST STORMS OFF LIKE A BABY SAYING HE'S GOING BACK TO IRELAND!
NOT BLEEDIN' LIKELY. HE'S LIVED IN AMERICA FOR HOW LONG?
JESUS, THERE'S ABSOLUTELY NOTHING ON T.V.!
WELL, EITHER WAY, MR. B IS STILL DEFINITELY SINGLE. MAYBE THERE'S HOPE FOR ME YET!
OH, WAIT, HERE'S SOMETHING.
WHAT THE HELL...?
WHAT IS THAT? IT LOOKS SORT OF FAMILIAR, BLEU!
NOOOOO! WHY GOD, WHYYYY?!?! AIIIEEE!
THOSE BOYS ARE SO DEAD.
AH, YOUTH. THE END!

absolute beginners

HI, THERE.
WE'VE RECEIVED A FEW COMPLAINTS THAT OUR MORONIC CREATOR CHYNNA HAS NEGLECTED TO REINTRODUCE US PROPERLY, SO THE CAST OF BLUE MONDAY DECIDED TO REMEDY THE SITUATION.
WE APOLOGIZE FOR THE CONFUSION. ENJOY!
SOUNDTRACK: HUMAN LEAGUE "MIRROR MAN"
HEY, CLOVER CONNELLY! WHAT'S UP?
HOY, BLEU L. FINNEGAN! I'M JUST WAITIN' FOR...
...ALAN WALSH AND VICTOR GOMEZ TO SHOW UP!
REALLY, CLOVER?
YES, BLEU!
AND LOOK! IT'S ERIN O'NEILL!
HI, BLEU! HI, CLOVER!
HI, ERIN!
... AND RISSA MEADE IS HERE, TOO!
HI, BLEU, CLOVER, AND ERIN!
HI, RISSA!
UH-OH, BLEU. DON'T LOOK NOW, BUT...
MR. BISHOP IS WALKING TO CLASS! (as if you didn't know.)
OOH, MR. BISHOP!
HIYA!
BUT WHERE'S MONKEYBOY?
RIGHT HERE IN THE TREE! HEY, BLEU, CLOVER, ALAN, VICTOR, ERIN, RISSA AND MR. BISHOP!
DON'T FORGET TOM, PATRICK, AND TRAVIS!
HEY, BLEU, CLOVER, ALAN, VICTOR, ERIN, RISSA, MR. BISHOP AND MONKEYBOY!
HEY!!!!!!!
HEY, MONKEYBOY!
ALRIGHTY, THEN! WE HOPE THIS HAS HELPED A BIT! THANKYOUVERYMUCH!

The following pages contain designs for the main characters originally intended as guides for a flash animation series that never was fully realized, thankfully.

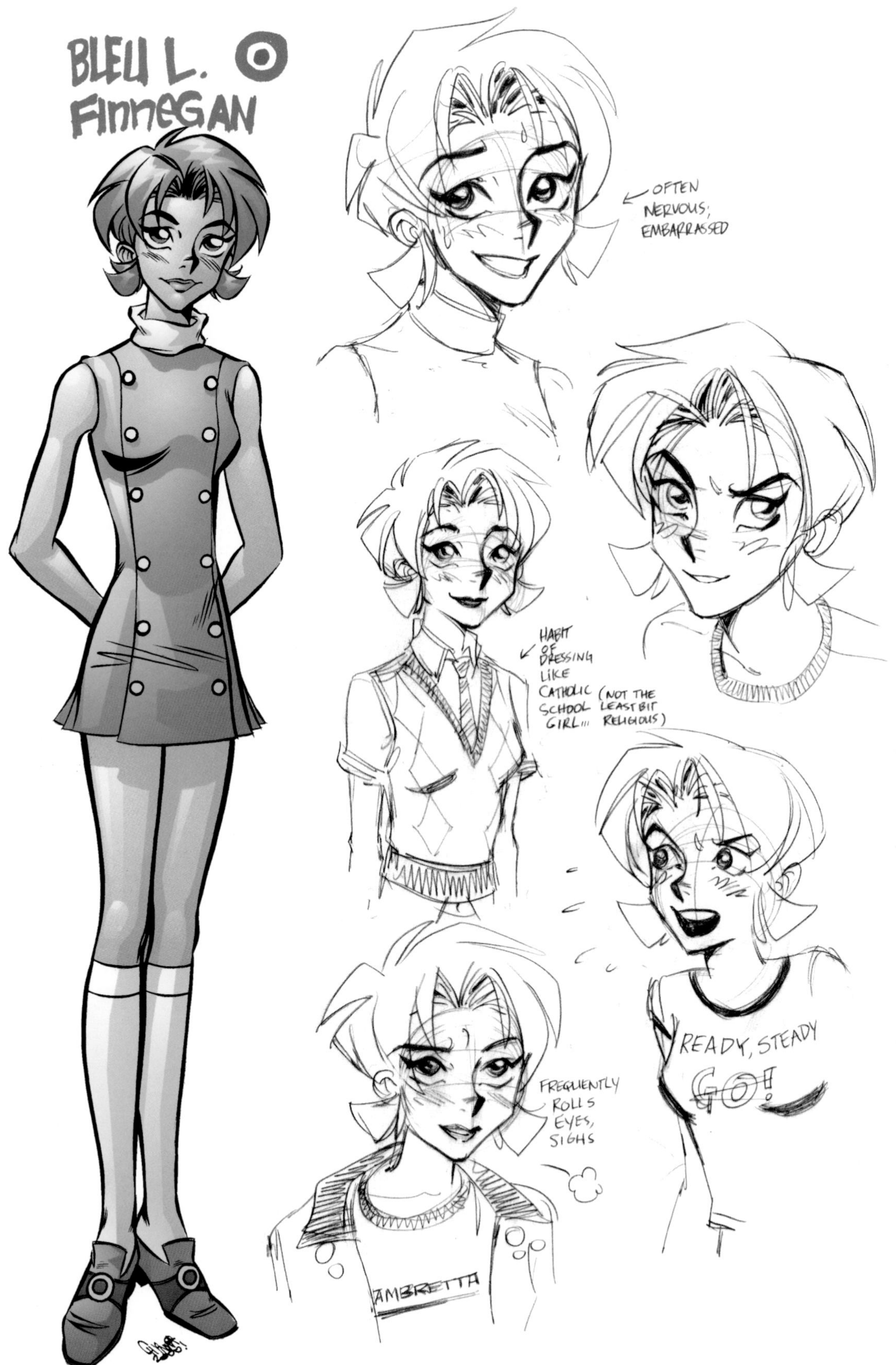

CLOVER CONNELLY
THE CRAMPS
APPEARS BARELY ABLE TO TOLERATE ANYONE'S COMPANY
ABOUT READY TO CRACK AND GIVE SOMEONE A GOOD SMACKING ABOUT
@&$*
@"%
RAMON
GIRL LOVES A SHOUTING MATCH
XPLOITED
2000

VICTOR GOMEZ
← PERV FACE (PROBABLY GOT A PANTY SHOT OR SOMETHING)
← THINKS HE'S A LADYKILLER!
A MORE QUIET MOMENT?
HA HA HA HA
NYC SKA

Typical Leer, Probably daydreaming about one of the girls
ALMOST ALWAYS IN PARKA UNLESS INDOORS (OR Summer)
even then...
UNION JACK PATCH LEFT SLEEVE
CLARKES
BACK O' JACKET
THE KINKS
DEDICATED FOLLOWER OF FASHION.
ALAN WALSH

ERIN O'NEILL
INFORMATION SOCIETY
ALWAYS WEARS HEADBAND
LECTURING
YAWN
OFTEN ACTS BORED OR TIRED
PERKY ERIN

Process Sketchbook

These are a few thumbnails from the early stages of *Absolute Beginners*. Typically, Chynna will write the rough draft of a comic and then sketch the thumbnails. Dialogue is added along the way as gags are worked out visually, and the second draft of the script is adjusted to reflect any changes. The final draft of the script comes after pencils and inks are laid down, where more changes inevitably occur. It's all a part of the long, convoluted process of creating *Blue Monday*!

BM:AB
PG. 18
CHARGE!
TAP
FOKS.
GOOOOOAL!!
GOOOOAL
I was wondering what he was doing just standin there like an idiot
dude!
We can't have em
Beat us 80 to nothing!
I have an idea!
Yeah!

Page 21 BM AB
What the hell's wrong with me lately?
Can't get my mind off...
Oh man... I couldn't be...
Not with her.
smaller
NO WAY.
No, I don't care what she thinks.
Classifieds
You think?
HAVE I REALLY BEEN THAT BLIND?
THAT'S IT!
What's it?

Page 22 BM AB
HAHA
SLAM
OH MY GOD?!
OH MY GOD!!!
HOP

Page 23 BM AB
BAMBAMB
AAA!
How could you?!
OKAY OKAY! Geez!
FUCKERS!!

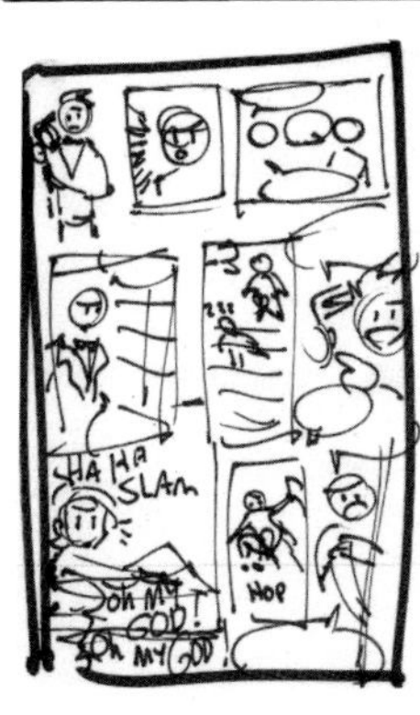
HA HA
SLAM
OH MY GOD!
OH MY GOD
HOP

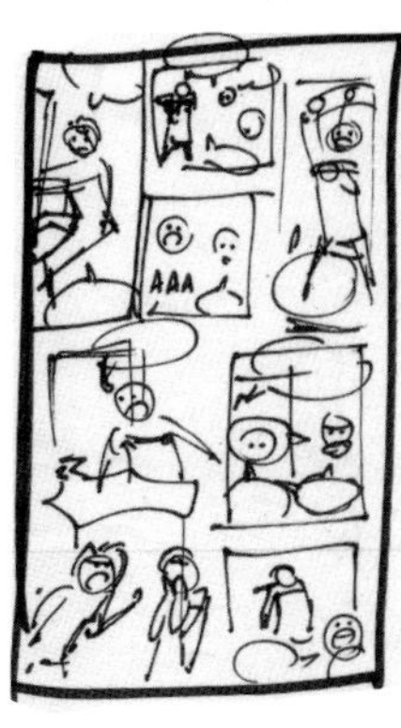
AAA

blue monday
RUDIE CAN'T FAIL
LOOK MOM... NO HEAD!
MODS
BUF!

Chynna Clugston Flores was born and raised in Fresno, California. Near the end of her freshman year at Roosevelt School of the Arts she went to live in a podunk town in the Sierra Nevadas where she ended up attending Yosemite High School in the early nineties and subsequently meeting a handful of misfit weirdos inspiring *Blue Monday* at sixteen. After living in San Diego for nearly twenty years, she is back in the land of tarantulas, toads and rattlesnakes, constantly remembering why she left in the first place. (She likes the tarantulas and toads, but the snakes not so much.) (Or, say, the high number of bigots.)

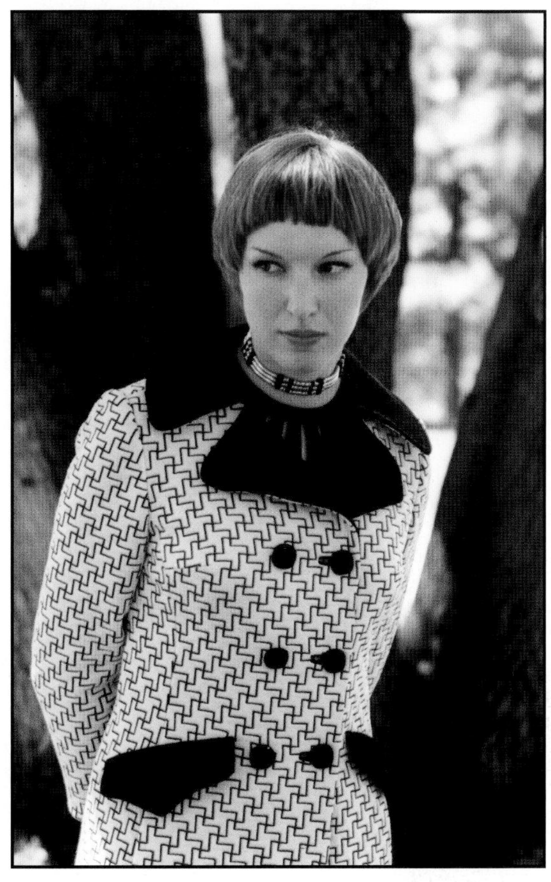

Chynna, circa the creation of *Absolute Beginners*

Chynna has been drawing and writing comics professionally since 1994 and has, for some inexplicable reason, stuck with it. She has worked with BOOM!, DC, Lion Forge, Oni Press, Marvel, Dark Horse, Slave Labor as well as working as an illustrator for books, magazines, ad companies, and as a writer, assistant editor and colorist. Most recently she was the writer for the hit crossover *Lumberjanes/Gotham Academy*, the artist and writer on a short story featuring Deadpool for the *Gwenpool Holiday Special Merry Mix Up* from Marvel, as well as some work on DC's *Shade the Changing Girl*. Chynna's original creator-owned series *Scooter Girl* will be available in color in Winter 2016, also through Image Comics.

Dedicated to the memory of Marty Nissen.

Special thanks to: Image Comics, Eric Stephenson, Jordie Bellaire, Ian Shaughnessy, Jamie S. Rich, Sean Konot, Steven Birch, Keith Wood, Drew Gill & Jon Flores.

Jordie Bellaire is a colorist who has worked on many titles with many publishers. Her credits include *Pretty Deadly, Nowhere Men, Moon Knight, Injection, The Autumnlands, They're Not Like Us, The X-Files, Vision,* and others. In 2016 she won her second Eisner award for Best Colorist. She lives in Ireland with her famous cat, Buffy.